THE HOUSEHOLD CARNIVORE

THE HOUSEHOLD CARNIVORE

How To Feed Your Cat A Raw Diet

Susan S. Collins

Copyright © 2007 by Susan S. Collins.

ISBN: Hardcover   978-1-4257-5166-1
            Softcover   978-1-4257-5164-7

Address inquiries to:

Susan S. Collins
susan.collins20@verizon.net

All rights reserved. No part of this book may be reproduced or transmitted in any form or by any means, electronic or mechanical, including photocopying, recording, or by an informational storage and retrieval system, without the written permission of the author.

This book was printed in the United States of America.

Disclaimer

This book has been written and is intended for informational purposes only. The reader accepts that the author is not giving any veterinary medical advice. The reader is responsible for seeking veterinary medical advice from a qualified veterinarian related to applying the information presented here. The author assumes no responsibility for errors, inaccuracies, omissions, or any other inconsistencies and cannot be held responsible for any loss or damages resulting from information contained within this book.

To order additional copies of this book, contact:
Xlibris Corporation
1-888-795-4274
www.Xlibris.com
Orders@Xlibris.com

CONTENTS

Acknowledgements 9
Preface: A Note from the Author 11

Section 1: Introduction—Why A Raw Diet? 15
1. Why a Raw Diet?
2. What's Wrong With Cooked Cat Food?
3. The Purpose of this Book

Section 2: How to Feed a Raw Diet 23
1. Essential Principles
   A. First Things
   B. Four Feeding Options
2. Proportions to aim for
3. Making Your Own Cat Food
   A. Cat Food Recipe for Option 3: *Homemade*
   B. Preparing the Alternate Raw Meaty Bone and Meat Meals for Option 2: *Commercial plus RMB* and for Option 3b: *Homemade plus RMB*
   C. Implementing Option 4: RMB Rotation
4. The Feeding Process
   A. Amounts to Feed
   B. Adapting the System for Kittens
   C. Making the System Work
5. Making the Switch
   A. Going Cold Turkey
   B. Dealing with Refusals to Eat
6. Keeping Track of Your Practices and Progress
7. Finding and Choosing Meat Sources
8. Fears and Concerns
   A. Issues Concerning Feeding Bones
   B. Bacteria and Parasites
9. Conclusion

Section 3: Ingredient Guide 69
1. Meat, Bones, and Vegetables
2. Supplements
3. Final Note on Ingredients

Appendix: Resources 75
1. Annotated Bibliography
2. Some Web-Based Resources
3. Endnotes

This book is dedicated to my two cats—
Clarence and Rosalind—
and to my two dogs—Nellie and Macduff—who have
taught me more than I ever could have imagined . . .
and to my wonderful husband, Chris, who put up with me
as I learned.

Acknowledgements

I am grateful to the devoted care and assistance of Dr. Monique Maniet of Veterinary Holistic Care in Bethesda, Maryland, who gave me and my animals considerable attention as we learned how to implement the raw diet. She encouraged me to write this book to share with others what we had learned. She also reviewed and edited this book for me, provided opportunties for me to give seminars on raw feeding at her clinic, and her staff was very helpful. I am also grateful to her associate, Dr. Carol Lundquist, who shared with me her experiences and urged me to complete this book. Most of all, I am indebted to my husband, Chris, who—in spite of initial doubts—has supported and continues to tirelessly support our adventures in raw feeding.
I am so very grateful to him for his careful editing and loving encouragement.

Preface

A Note from the Author

This book arose from a series of seminars that I gave to help other people become familiar with the raw diet and help them determine whether they wanted to feed it to their companion animals. I make no claims to be an animal scientist or nutritionist. I am simply an animal lover and caretaker who figured out on my own how to feed a raw diet to cats and dogs. It was a challenging process. My intention in writing this book is to make that process a little easier—and hopefully a lot less angst ridden—for others than it was for me.

I began feeding a raw diet to one of our dogs in the winter of 2000. She was an extremely immune compromised rescue dog who had been badly beaten and starved. No commercial food had helped alleviate her severe skin, ear, and coat problems, so eventually I discovered Dr. Richard Pitcairn's recipes and began making my own food for her. I was afraid, however, to use raw meat, so instead made tremendous pots of "porridge" with oatmeal, cooked meat and vegetables, and some very complicated supplement mixes. This entailed a lot of time consuming work, but did not do much to improve our dog's condition.

Fortunately, one day some "kind" purveyor of supplements with whom I spoke chided me for cooking my dog's food. I was so embarrassed that I got on the Internet and started reading about raw feeding. I ordered Dr. Billinghurst's first book and devoured it, but still was uncertain. Through a roundabout series of conversations, I discovered a veterinarian who raised whippets and had fed her dogs a raw diet for five years. After a two hour consultation with her, I finally felt confident enough to start feeding my dog a raw diet.

The adjustment was a hard one—but only for me! My dog took to raw food about as readily as you can imagine. She loved it! Crunching bones and eating raw meat was the best thing in the world! Within a couple of weeks, her coat was looking better, and within a few months, she seemed like a changed dog. She put on muscle where she had never had it, gained energy and seemed happier. Her skin changed from bright pink and smelly to normal pink and free of infection. She still had yeast in her ears, but that has been cleared up too over time as her immune system has become stronger. We were able to reduce her thyroid medication nearly by a third. And she has been infection and parasite free for the last six summers.

For me, though, it took some real work to prepare meals and get over the stress of worrying about what might happen. I worried about bacteria, about bones in her system, and most importantly, about whether I was feeding a "balanced" diet so that she would get all the nutrition she needed. To ease my concern, I read everything I could get my hands on and even took a veterinary technician class to develop better understanding of how these creatures work.

Fortunately, nothing did happen, so eventually I relaxed and realized I could do it. We settled into a routine that continues to this day and we now have a second dog thriving on a raw diet. I have learned a tremendous amount and have achieved a level of comfort with experimenting to understand what really works best for my animals.

About six months after beginning to feed a raw diet to our dog, I began feeding our two cats this way. I had been reluctant to try because there was even less guidance available for feeding cats a raw diet than there was for dogs. After a second late night trip to the emergency vet with my rescued feral cat bleeding in his urine, I decided that it was then or never—the dry food I had been feeding him was causing crystals that were blocking his urinary tract and could potentially kill him. Either I could feed a specially made commercial canned food for urinary tract problems, sold through veterinarians, or switch to raw. It was a no-brainer.

I began making the recipe provided on the Feline Future website and within two weeks, our sick cat was totally back to normal and has been thriving ever since. Originally, I followed the directions exactly; later, I modified the recipe to account for what I learned from other sources and came to believe was right for my cats and what I saw that they liked and disliked. I continued to read and learn about cats and nutrition, and I discovered how different cats are from dogs! I ground up very fresh, pasture raised chickens and other meats to make their food, and they began to thrive. Eventually, I realized that I could make my life even simpler by feeding whole pieces of food and letting them do much of the grinding themselves—all I had to do was make sure they got balance over time and that they could chew the pieces. They couldn't be happier or healthier now, and it couldn't be simpler for me.

I was very fortunate to have an extremely supportive holistic veterinarian, Dr. Monique Maniet of Veterinary Holistic Care in Bethesda, MD, who encouraged me to pursue this style of feeding for all my animals. When I began feeding a raw diet, she was not yet advocating it regularly to her clients. She started to gain more and more interest and pursued more and more information, so that now she is recommending the raw diet to many of her clients. She now sells Billinghurst's most recent book and offers a variety of frozen raw food from her clinic.

Because I had figured out how to feed both cats and dogs a raw home made diet, Dr. Maniet and I agreed that others might benefit if I shared what I had learned. I've held several seminars in her clinic for interested animal caretakers and given one-on-one consultations to help people develop their own feeding systems that suited their lifestyles and their animals' needs. I have since held seminars at other vets' offices as well.

In the process of doing these things, it became even more apparent to me that this is not a difficult thing to do, but that it takes a change of attitude toward animal feeding. Many people are reluctant because it is not a conventional practice these days, so they wonder whether it can be the right way to go. Most veterinarians do not have any experience feeding raw food—they aren't taught it in vet school and they don't practice it themselves—so they are often suspicious, at best, and sometimes downright combative toward it. Because there have been so many recent scares about bacterial contamination in human foods, many people, including veterinarians, are fearful that raw meat will hurt their animals. Most veterinarians have at least one horror story about bones stuck in an animal's digestive system, usually a dog who has found a cooked chicken bone outside. They are understandably leery of the idea of feeding bones and do not understand the difference between raw and cooked bone. As a result, most raw feeders do not have a vet who knows about the diet, let alone supports it.

I believe that all that people really need is a little guidance to help figure out what to feed, in what amounts, and how to develop a system that can be integrated into their lives while giving their animals the nutrition they need. They also need some comfort that this is not a dangerous way to feed their animals—that, on the contrary, the experience with this way of feeding leads to excellent health and longevity.

This book, then, is intended to help others to learn from my experience, to get started feeding a raw diet, to get comfortable with a system, and to have confidence that they can make good decisions about how to care for their furry companions. My hope is that it will give readers a realistic view into what is involved and will allay any fears that are not truly justified. Most of all, I hope that it will help everyone who reads it to decide how to feed their animals best in the context of their own, individual needs and values.

Happy feeding!

Susan Collins
January 2007

Section 1

Introduction—Why A Raw Diet?

1. Why a Raw Diet?

Let your cat answer this question: what would he eat if he were hunting for his dinner?

He'll tell you that he would catch mice, chipmunks, sparrows, crickets, and a variety of other small rodents, birds, and insects. Not only that, he'll tell you that he would eat almost every part of them: their flesh of course, and also some of their fur or feathers, most of their internal organs, much of their intestinal tract, and most importantly, their bones. All he'd leave would be the occasional beak, skull, and a few other remnants.

And everything would be RAW and *very* fresh.

So why feed your cat a raw diet? To provide your domesticated carnivore with a natural diet that most closely resembles what his instincts would tell him to eat if he were fending for himself.

Of course, that doesn't completely answer the question. The real question is, In what ways will a raw diet that imitates the diet of a wild feline (given the constraints of modern food production) improve your domestic cat's health, vitality, and longevity?

The answers are numerous. Feeding a raw diet focused on raw meaty bones will help your cat . . .

. . . Develop a strong immune system that will keep disease at bay, minimizing or eliminating skin and other sensitivities and allergies;

... Have strong teeth, bones, and coat that support long life and vitality;
... Easily maintain a healthy weight, which is a significant determinant of long term health;
... Eliminate most digestive tract problems;
... Keep teeth clean and breath fresh, enhancing systemic health and eliminating the need for costly tooth cleaning at the vet's office under anesthesia;
... Keep ears healthy and clean naturally, eliminating the need for painful and difficult cleaning;
... Reduce and even eliminate the attraction to fleas and other parasites;
... Increase energy levels and moderate extreme demeanors;
... Reduce the potential for diseases related to urinary tract, digestive, and other physiological systems;
... Lessen the seriousness of a wide variety of conditions, including urinary tract problems and FUS, immune mediated conditions, respiratory conditions, etc.
... Reduce the amount of toxins being introduced into your cat's system.

All these effects of a raw diet are easily achievable and will save you time and money in the long run as you decrease non-routine visits to the veterinarian's office. Although every cat will be different, and although diet is not the only factor affecting health, the experience of raw feeders is that the diet reduces the likelihood that your cat will develop serious health problems that will diminish his and your quality of life in the long run. On the contrary—no matter what his genetic disposition, the raw diet, properly fed, will increase the chances that your cat will live a long, healthy life as your companion.

2. What's Wrong With Cooked Cat Food?

Your cat is naturally a carnivore. You can tell this easily by taking a quick look at his teeth: they are ALL pointed and very sharp, perfect for ripping and tearing skin, muscle, and bone. None of his teeth have flat surfaces like human molars or the teeth of ruminants (e.g., horses, sheep, cows,) which are intended to grind grasses, grains, and vegetables into small enough pieces to begin digestion.

A little closer examination that has been done by animal scientists[1] has shown that, unlike humans, cats do not have digestive enzymes in their saliva—they tear animal prey into small enough pieces to swallow and then let their stomachs, which are much more acidic than ours, begin the hard work of digesting what is mostly protein and fat. This highly acidic stomach environment is able to kill bacteria and other things that, typically, are harmful to humans. All this suggests that we can not apply human standards to our consideration of the nutritional needs of cats.

This book does not intend to provide a comprehensive explanation of the scientific foundations of feline nutrition. Neither will it go into great detail about reasons to avoid feeding cooked food or to catalogue the evils of commercial dry and canned cat food. You can read more about these topics in many other sources, some of which are noted in the resources section at the back of this book.

Suffice it to say that cooked food—whether highly processed food bought at the grocery store, pet store, a high priced specialty store, or from a respectable vet, or home-prepared cooked food—all will lack some critical nutrients that most readily support your cat's health.

Most importantly, as a true carnivore, your cat is meant to eat a diet very high in protein, along with considerable amounts of fat but with very little carbohydrate. Your cat is also meant to eat food that is 65-75% moisture. In contrast, most dry foods are roughly 10% moisture. Cat food made with large amounts of cereal grains, which are cheap and readily available, will not provide the optimal amount or types of essential building blocks to promote health. Although commercial foods provide a minimum nutrition to support life, they do not necessarily promote *health*.

Cats thrive on a diet that is roughly 90-95% animal matter—meat, bones, internal organs, indigestible fiber (aka fur, feathers, claws, etc.)—and only 5-10% vegetable matter—for a cat hunting for himself, that vegetable matter would primarily come from ingesting the prey's intestinal tract. Since cats have a short digestive tract, they can only digest vegetable matter that is generally already "predigested".[2] Unless a mouse or bird ate grain, cats living in the wild would not eat any cereal grains at all.

The composition of commercial cat foods differ dramatically from the composition of the diet a feline hunter would eat. Dry cat food is typically 70 to 80% carbohydrate, turning upside down the proportions of protein, fat, and carbohydrates in the cat's diet. Most recipes for home made cat food also use substantial amounts of cooked cereal grains as their base. The proteins in these grains do not contain the same quality of building blocks that animal-based protein sources do, meaning that cats are not getting everything they need from grain-based food.

Some veterinarians and animal researchers believe that this over-reliance on grains as a source of nutrition has led to the development of high rates of digestive tract diseases like irritable bowel disease and autoimmune diseases like diabetes. Although little research has been done in this arena, anecdotal evidence has shown consistently that moving away from a high carbohydrate diet to one that is high in animal protein significantly improves the condition of cats, even those who have already developed diseases.

The biggest problem with cooked food, whether commercially made or home made, is that the cooking transforms valuable nutrients in ways that make them less "bioavailability", meaning that the cat's system can not readily access and use them. Cooking changes the chemical composition of the flesh and bone, so that essential amino acids, essential fatty acids, vitamins, trace minerals, and other important nutrients are changed chemically. When this happens, they can not be used as readily by your cat's body to generate or sustain his body's needs.

Cooking destroys live enzymes, amino acids, and vitamins in the raw food, and changes the composition of minerals present. Enzymes serve partly to help the animal digest the food and unlock the nutrients therein and support the cat's biological systems. Amino acids are the building blocks of protein that the cat's body uses to build strong muscles, tissues, and organs. Vitamins and minerals are essential contributors to the proper functioning of all metabolic systems. Hence, the less available these are the cat's system, the lower the quality of his physical well being.

Most importantly, cooked bones are not easily consumable by cats. This is why cooked commercial food includes calcium supplements. The process of cooking bone hardens it, making it very brittle and likely to splinter, and locks the minerals in place and so that they are not bioavailable. This poses a great problem because all mammals need calcium and phosphorous in the right proportions to support skeletal structure, healthy skin and hair, and most other vital systems. Muscle meat has high quantities of phosphorous, but very little calcium. If a cat does not either eat bone raw or receive supplemental calcium on a regular basis, he will eventually suffer from severe skeletal problems.[3]

Feeding raw meaty bones from relatively small animals—which is naturally soft and can be chewed by cats—is the safest way to ensure that your cat is getting the right proportions of these essential minerals, as well as essential amino and fatty acids, which must be acquired from food because the cat's body does not produce them on its own. In addition to eating meat and bone in their most digestible and nutritionally dense forms, the process of chewing raw meat with bone provides exercise and psychological satisfaction for your carnivore.

Cat food companies and home-made cat food cooks deal with these issues by adding back nutrients to their food in order to satisfy the minimum nutritional needs of your cat. They add back vitamins and minerals, as well as adding calcium supplements to ensure that cats receive enough calcium to support bone and tissue growth, among other critical physical systems. Commercial food producers must also add preservatives, and often add flavor enhancers in order to convince your cat that the food is palatable.

Commercially made dry and canned cat food made with human grade ingredients and natural supplements and preservatives are more and more readily available. However, no cooked food can ever provide the nutrition that food in its raw state can, and no food high in carbohydrates can imitate what your cat would obtain through instinct-driven hunting.

3. The Purpose of this Book

The raw diet advocated in this book follows the recommendations of Dr. Ian Billinghurst, who rejuvenated the idea of feeding companion animals a diet consisting largely of raw meaty bones. His "BARF" diet—Bones and Raw Food, or Biologically Appropriate Raw Food—has been used extensively by dog owners around the world since the publication of his first book in 1993. Until he wrote his more recent book that briefly discusses feeding cats a raw diet, there was very little written about feeding this diet to cats.

The recommendations put forth here also rely heavily on the research and recipes made public by Feline Future, a research foundation dedicated to improving feline nutrition and health. They have been one of the very few—if not the only!—organizations exclusively emphasizing research on nutrition and health of cats. This book intends to fill a gap somewhat by helping individuals put into practice some of the principles developed by these scientists.

No one argues that our house cats should hunt if we can keep them inside. After all, there are rabid possums, fights with other cats who may not be healthy, cars, and many other significant health hazards. But we can try to imitate the diet the cat would provide for himself naturally.

You are probably wondering how you can possibly replicate the diet of a wild cat. This all sounds awfully difficult, you are probably thinking.

That's really why this book has been written—to show you that it is not only possible to imitate the diet of a feline hunter, it is possible to do so in a way that comfortably suits your tastes, lifestyle, and wallet. This book acknowledges that it may be difficult for vegetarians to handle raw meat, but hopes that they will find comfort in knowing they are feeding their little carnivores the best, most natural, most species appropriate diet possible.

This book is not intended to sell you on the idea of raw feeding. There are several other excellent sources for learning about the nutrition behind a raw diet that consists largely of raw meat and bones; several of them are listed at the end of this book, and there are innumerable valuable sources available for you to peruse on the Internet. You are *strongly* encouraged to read as much as you can to learn why this book promotes the diet as a critical component to promoting health and longevity in your companion, and then to make decisions that suit your own desires and needs.

This book *is* intended to be a "how-to" guide so that, once you decide it is right for you, you can feed your cat using this natural approach without worry that you are jeopardizing his health. The chapters that follow will show you, in the most practical of terms, how to make the raw diet work for both you and your cat.

You will find just a few simple rules of thumb to keep in mind, recipes for making your own food, options that involve more or less work on your part and more or less expense, so that you can choose the approach that best suits your busy life. You will be guided on amounts to start feeding your cat, how to keep track of what you are feeding, and how to make modifications as you learn. Finally, you will have at your fingertips a list of valuable resources for learning more and for purchasing products that you may want to use.

Most of all, this book is intended to help you to be able to put this diet into practice. Just like any other regimen you want to follow, it will take a little getting used to; once you develop some familiarity with the steps and gain comfort in using them, you will undoubtedly find feeding this health-promoting diet easy and fulfilling. Most of all, you will know that you are giving your cat the best you can to help him live a long, happy, healthy life. Who knows—becoming more attentive to the nutritional needs of your cat may even help you to eat better!

Section 2

How to Feed a Raw Diet

1. Essential Principles

Feeding a raw diet is a matter of making choices. Every choice you make will be related to your preferences, your cat's reactions, and your budget.

This chapter presents you with four options for feeding your cat. It outlines the pros and cons of choosing each alternative. In each case, there are tradeoffs among the amount of time and effort it takes to prepare, how expensive it is, the tastes of your cat, and the health benefits for your cat. These options are presented as a way to help you decide what is most appropriate for you given your constraints and what is most important to you.

No single choice is "right"; you do not need to choose one exclusively (you can mix and match as needed,) nor are they the only options for healthfully feeding your cat a raw diet. Treat them as starting points for making your decision and adjust to fit the needs of you and your cat as you learn more about the components of the diet, yourself, and your companion.

A. First Things

There really is not that much to remember about this diet—here are some basic principles that will serve you well over time as you become more and more comfortable with feeding your cat this way:

- You achieve nutritional balance over time by feeding a wide variety of meats, bones, and organ meats—there is no need to create a "complete and balanced" meal every time, but variety over time is essential because different meats have different building blocks—so the more variety, the more likely your cat will get everything he needs.
- Feed the best you can afford, given the other demands in your life, and realize that no matter what that entails, it will be better than feeding grain-based, highly processed food.
- Feed twice a day, making food available for a limited time (half hour or hour)—follow natural eating patterns and take advantage of hunger.
- Let your cats do more of the work than you do, i.e., cut or grind as little as you feel comfortable with doing and let them chew as much as they will do! Remember, though, that sometimes refusal to eat can be eliminated simply by cutting pieces smaller.

- Use meat that is very fresh and keep vegetable proportions low, or cats are likely to reject the food; remember that less processed or handled meat will be fresher, so grinding meat yourself or cutting it into small pieces may be preferable to pre-ground meat.
- Cats are animals of habit—be patient as you introduce new foods.
- Most of the raw meaty bones you feed will, of necessity, come from poultry (and if possible, rabbit) because it is very difficult to cut or grind at home bones from larger animals, and cats simply can't chew bones that are too big. Don't worry about poultry being the dominant source for bones, but do vary the muscle meat you feed in order to ensure variety of protein sources. To the extent possible, vary the poultry raw meaty bones that you feed.
- Keep supplementation simple—remember that most of the nutrition comes from the food itself. If a cat has special needs, consult your veterinarian and be sure your doctor knows you are feeding a raw diet. If your vet is not supportive, consider finding a holistic vet who is.
- Remember, every cat is different: they have different tastes, different metabolisms, different underlying health conditions, and different personalities—stay open to experimentation and use your judgment by carefully observing what happens.

B. Four Feeding Options

The first obvious question about feeding a raw diet is how to do it. This section considers four options for feeding your cat two meals per day. These options should give you enough structure to get started. In each case, "RMB" means "raw meaty bones". The options are as follow:

(1) **Commercial**: Feed only frozen raw food made commercially.
(2) **Commercial + RMB**: Alternate commercially made frozen raw food with meals of raw meaty bones and meat.
(3) **Homemade**: Make your own ground raw food following a recipe that includes everything needed for good nutrition; **(a) Homemade only**: feed only your homemade ground food, or **(b) Homemade + RMB**: alternate homemade ground food with meals of raw meaty bones and meat.
(4) **RMB Rotation**: Rotate meals of whole raw meaty bones and meat, occasionally including varying amounts of pulverized vegetables, organ meat, and supplements. Do so in a manner that creates balance over time.

Each of these options has advantages and disadvantages. Table I compares the pros and cons of each option so that you can consider which one makes the most sense for you and your cat.

Option 1: Commercial *Feed commercially made, frozen raw food at each meal*

Option 1 consists of feeding commercially prepared, frozen raw food at every meal. This option requires the preparer to purchase food, store it in a freezer, and take out food a couple of hours before meal time to defrost.

The advantage of option 1 is that it is very easy for the preparer, because it most resembles feeding conventional commercial cat food. One simply measures out the appropriate amount of defrosted food and serves. The preparer does not need to handle raw meat or put any ingredients together.

Typically, everything your cat needs is included in these frozen products: ground raw meaty bones, muscle meat, organs, vegetables, vitamins, minerals, Omega-3 fatty acids, and sometimes other supplements. Read ingredients carefully, however. Check to be sure that the manufacturer is grinding raw bone rather than simply adding calcium supplement. Some commercial producers sell both complete meals and products that consist solely of ground meat, bone, and organs. Depending on your taste and what your cat will eat, you can use the complete product or add your own vegetables and supplements to the meat/bone/organ ground food.

Using commercial products means you don't have to worry about balance over time because it's done for you. Your cat will be getting the most bioavailable sources of protein and fat with very little carbohydrates, the most natural sources and proportions of calcium and phosphorus, as well as enzymes and other nutrients needed for long term health.

If you travel frequently, you may want to use this option when you ask someone else to feed your cat for you. Not all boarding facilities are able to accommodate frozen food, however. A few producers of frozen raw food also offer freeze-dried versions that can be used as a good, if costly, alternative.

While this option is certainly the most convenient, it has some significant disadvantages. The primary disadvantage of choosing option 1 is that your cat does not have the opportunity to chew raw meaty bones, and therefore does not benefit from the tooth cleaning, exercise, and emotional support that arise from chewing bones.

In addition, just as with any commercial product, you have no control over the quality of the ingredients or the variety included in your cat's diet. Although the suppliers listed in the Appendix are generally reliable, you may prefer to have more control over both the quality and the variety in your cat's diet. And the decision may be out of your hands: many prepared frozen foods are rejected by cats, possibly because they include too many vegetables, because the meat is not fresh enough, or for some other reason only appreciated by feline sensibilities.

If you choose this option, you will need to locate a supplier, which may be easy or difficult depending on where you live, you will need to pay for shipping if no local suppliers are available, and you will definitely need freezer space to accommodate it. Finally, this is the most expensive option for feeding your cat a raw diet.

At this writing, there are many options for high quality, commercial frozen and freeze dried raw food. Sources for such food are readily found through the Internet, holistic animal well being magazines, holistic veterinarians, and boutique pet stores. Many commercially available frozen food producers make one recipe for both dogs and cats. While some cats are content to eat food that has vegetable content geared for dogs, many are not. In addition, some frozen foods seem to be made with fresher ingredients than others. Cats are much more picky about freshness than dogs are and will sometimes reject food that dogs find delicious. Therefore, it is recommended that you seek food specifically designed for cats and experiment with different varieties before stocking up.

Option 1 is by far the easiest and therefore, for people who are very busy, it is a practical solution that is far preferable to feeding cooked commercial food. Nevertheless, given the cost and the other drawbacks, you may want to continue reading about the other options and consider expanding into one of them later if and when it seems feasible for you.

Option 2: Commercial + RMB *Alternate commercial frozen raw food with raw meaty bone and meat meals*

Option 2 is particularly practical for someone who is very busy, yet able to take the time to include raw meaty bones and meat in the diet because of their tremendous health benefits. Ideally, one meal consists of the commercial product, the other meal consists of RMB or meat alone to ensure that your cat is getting the right proportion of bone to meat over time.

Like Option 1, this option eliminates the need to prepare and mix ingredients and eliminates concerns that you have included the right ingredients. All the work is done for you by the producers of the commercial product. At the same time, by alternating the commercial product with meals of raw meaty bones and meat, you are still able to give your cat the benefit of chewing.

You also have more opportunity to feed a wider variety of meat sources using this option, thereby increasing the likelihood that your cat has all his nutritional needs met. Different food sources have different chemical properties; in particular meat sources have different combinations and proportions of amino acids and fatty acids, among other nutrients that contribute to health. The more variety in the diet, the more likely your cat will have available those building blocks critical to peak health and longevity.

This option has some disadvantages in that it is neither completely carefree nor gives you complete control over ingredients. While it is easier than other options, it requires some forethought and planning to purchase ingredients for alternate meals and requires some time to prepare them. And while you can introduce variety through the alternate meals, you have no control over the quality or variety of the commercial product. This option also shares Option 1's disadvantages of being more expensive, and requiring that you find a distributor of a product that your cat will eat. In fact, if your cat doesn't like the frozen product, alternating meals is a problem, because he is likely to avoid the prepared food and wait for the next meal. Finally, you need freezer space for the food you purchase.

Table 1: Comparing Different Options for Feeding Cats a Raw Diet

Feeding Option*	Advantages	Disadvantages
Option 1: Commercial—Feed commercially made, frozen raw food at each meal	• Easiest alternative • Most similar to feeding cooked commercial food • Need not handle raw meat • Easily achieve balance over time • No special equipment needed • Least time consuming • Very easy for someone else to feed	• Many cats don't like the taste/smell of commercial products, so may be hard to find one your cat likes • No benefits from chewing raw meaty bones • Least control over ingredient quality, variety • Most expensive • Must have freezer space • Must find distributor
Option 2: Commercial + RMB—Alternate commercial frozen raw food with raw meaty bone and meat meals	• Very convenient • Provides benefits of chewing raw meaty bones • Some control over variety • Easily achieve balance over time • Easily switch to option 1 when very busy or someone else feeds	• Some time required to prepare alternate meals • Must handle raw meat • May be hard to find frozen food your cat likes • No control over ingredients in commercial product • More expensive than alternatives 3 and 4 • Must have freezer space • Must find distributor

Option 3a: **Homemade only**—Make your own raw cat food following a complete and balanced recipe and feed at each meal	• Complete control over ingredient quality, variety • Recipe easy to follow • Easily achieve balance over time • Once prepared, meals are very convenient to feed • Less expensive than options 1 or 2 • Relatively easy for someone else to feed	• Preparation of food takes time, equipment • Must handle raw meat • Must choose (a) grind bones or (b) use calcium supplement: (a) requires special equipment, effort; (b) may not be optimal way to provide calcium all the time • No tooth cleaning or psychological benefit from chewing action • Must have freezer space
Option 3b: **Homemade + RMB**—Alternate your home made raw cat food with raw meaty bone and meat meals	• Complete control over ingredient quality, variety • Once prepared, meals are relatively easy to feed • Provides best sources and forms of nutrients, especially calcium • Easily achieve balance over time • Provides benefits of chewing raw meaty bones • Less work to prepare over time than option 3a • Less expensive than options 1 and 2 • Provides peace of mind about giving everything necessary for health • Can easily shift to option 1 or 3a in very busy times or when someone else feeds • You learn what constitutes a healthy raw diet	• Preparation of home made food takes time • Some time required to prepare alternate meals • Must handle raw meat • Some special equipment needed • Must have freezer space

Option 4: RMB Rotation—Alternate raw meaty bone meals with meat meals, including vegetables, organs, eggs, and occasional supplements	• Easiest way to provide the best diet possible • Least time consuming option • Least expensive • Least amount of equipment needed • Have options to prepare meals as needed or prepare them in meal sized packages in freezer	• Must be very attentive to balancing food sources and supplements over time • Some time required to prepare meals • Cats may reject vegetables, vitamins, other components • Must handle raw meat every day, organ meat regularly • May need freezer space • May have to switch to option 1 or 3a when someone else feeds

*NOTE: All feeding options are based on feeding an adult cat two times per day; options will need to be modified for feeding kittens younger than six months old.

Option 3: Homemade *Make your own raw cat food following a complete and balanced recipe—feed at each meal or alternate with meals of raw meaty bones and meat*

Option 3 actually represents several options. The basis for this option is preparing your own, home made cat food based on a recipe that ensures you have all the necessary ingredients for a complete and balanced diet. (The recipe is provided in the next section.[4]) As with the previous two options, you can choose to feed this ground recipe exclusively, or you can choose to alternate it with meals of raw meaty bones and meat.

First, consider the advantages of making your own cat food: you have complete control over the quality of ingredients and the variety that you include in the food you make. This enables you to choose whether to purchase meat from naturally raised animals or from conventional sources.[5] You can control the freshness of the meat, and also adapt the food to the tastes of your animal as you learn about what he likes and dislikes.

In addition, the recipe is relatively easy to follow: all you need to do is purchase the ingredients, prepare them, mix them together, and then store them in small containers to be put in the freezer and defrosted as needed. Following the recipe makes it easy to be sure that you are not leaving something important out of your cat's diet. Concern about creating a nutritional deficiency is a frequent worry for new raw feeders and is eliminated by following the recipe.

Once the recipe is prepared and frozen, feeding is very easy and convenient for you or someone else by defrosting the frozen mixture in advance of feeding. Finally, preparing food yourself from whole meats, vegetables, and supplements is much less expensive than purchasing commercially made raw food.

There are, of course, some disadvantages to this option. The primary disadvantage is that it takes time to purchase the ingredients and prepare the home made food. This involves handling raw meat and cutting up organ meat, and may involve grinding bones as well. If you decide to grind bones, you will need special equipment. Freezer space will be essential for storing, although it is typically easier to store small containers than large packages of commercial frozen food.

These considerations are much less significant for someone who likes to cook and has the time to do so than for someone who is not inclined to cook for themselves. If you typically are inclined to cook, you are likely to find this option merely an extension of what you already do for yourself and your family.

Should you choose to make your own cat food, you can either feed it exclusively or alternate it with meals of raw meaty bones and meat. These options are analogous to Option 1 and Option 2, and share the same considerations: if you feed only ground food, your cat will not benefit from chewing raw meaty bones and whole pieces of meat. While it is simpler to feed the ground food exclusively, you may choose to use the alternate meals as well to provide the benefits of clean teeth, exercise, and emotional support.

One significant benefit to making your own food using the recipe is that you will become increasingly familiar with the essential elements of the raw diet. For many people, this knowledge gives them peace of mind that they are, indeed, providing the best diet possible for one's cat. This greater appreciation for the raw diet may give you confidence in your choice as well as helping you develop more ideas for additional feeding options.

Option 4: RMB Rotation *Alternate raw meaty bone meals with meat meals, including vegetables, organs, eggs, and occasional supplements*

Option 4 is for the more advanced raw feeder. The idea is that you feed exactly the same ingredients that are included in the recipe, but you feed them in larger pieces and let your cat do the work of chewing. Of course, this is successful only if your cat cooperates and agrees to eat everything you give him! If he does, this option can make the raw diet even easier for you once you have achieved peace of mind regarding the ingredients by first using Option 3 or a similar approach.

The greatest advantage to this option is that *you* don't do the work, your cat does. All you have to do is think about what you want to feed over the course of a week or two and then purchase it and cut the food into the biggest pieces your cat will eat. This is both the least time consuming and the least expensive option for you. You can either prepare meals in packages and store in the freezer, defrosting as needed, or buy fresh food on a regular basis and feed directly from the refrigerator.

The disadvantages of this option are that you must pay much closer attention to what you are feeding in order to be sure that you are not leaving out critical components of the diet. In addition, cats are notoriously finicky—if your cat refuses to eat an important component of the diet, you may have to develop some tricks by combining those components with things he will eat. This option also means you will be handling raw meat every day and organ meat on a regular basis. Finally, this is not generally an option that other people will readily adapt to, so if you ask someone else to feed your cat, you may need to rely on home made or commercial ground raw food during that time.

Conclusion about the Options:

No one of these options is "the best" way to feed your cat. Having read through the pros and cons, trust your gut feeling about what you want to do and what you think will best serve both you and your cat as things currently stand. Realize that if you have more than one cat, your time and cost will increase proportionately. Do the best you can given your time and financial resources, and realize that you can always try another option if the one first chosen doesn't work, or try a more labor intensive option after you have become comfortable with an easier one, or go back to a simpler one when new demands arise in your life.

Although each of these options carries a price tag in terms of your money and your time, keep in mind that the health benefits will reduce the amount of time and money you spend in your veterinarian's office addressing preventable disease. Moreover, the time and money invested in feeding your cat will increase the likelihood that he will live a long, healthy life.

The sections that follow describe exactly how to make your own cat food, along with options for you to choose from, and how to make the alternate raw meaty bone and meat meals that you can use either with commercial food (Option 2: Commercial + RMB) or the home made food (Option 3b: Homemade + RMB). First, some proportions are given to offer you rules of thumb to follow as helpful guidelines. Following these sections is a description of how to implement Option 4: RMB Rotation.

2. Proportions to aim for

Anxiety over feeding a raw diet can be reduced significantly by keeping in mind some basic proportions of ingredients. Some simple proportions to remember will ease your concerns about whether you are providing sufficient balance over time. If you are feeding roughly in these proportions over the course of a week or two, your cat will be getting everything he needs. Even if you are feeding a commercial product exclusively, it is helpful to keep these proportions in mind to evaluate the results your cat is experiencing with any product.

The following proportions are guidelines only and should be adjusted as necessary for your animal. However, they provide a useful starting point and benchmark for you as you learn:

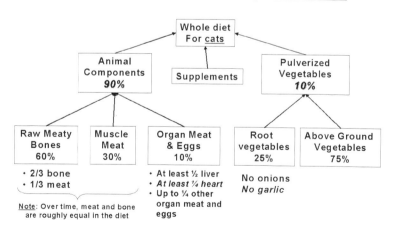

Proportions to Aim For In Feeding Cats a Raw Diet

Some important things to note are as follow:

- A Raw Meaty Bone (RMB) is between 1/2 and 2/3 bone (including cartilage). Here are some chicken RMB:

- Over time, meat and bone will be roughly equal in the diet. Think about the proportions of meat to bone in a chipmunk or sparrow if you need a frame of reference.
- Organs should include primarily liver and heart. Liver is an important source of Vitamin A. Taurine, an essential amino acid that your cat can only obtain through his food[6], is found in large quantities in raw heart. While raw meat also contains taurine, heart has much higher concentrations. Taurine does not stand up well to heat, which is why it must be added back to cooked food.
- Cats should not be fed onions or garlic, as they can cause blood disorders. Most other vegetables are fine; however, most cats dislike strong smells and prefer milder vegetables.

3. Making Your Own Cat Food

For anyone who has made any of the grain based home made cat food recipes available, the raw diet will seem remarkably simple. And it is. The only ingredients in the raw diet are raw meaty bones, raw muscle meat, organ meat, pulverized vegetables, eggs, and a few supplements. This *is* simple.

The following recipe has been developed by integrating the work of veterinarians, researchers, and practitioners who have developed raw feeding regimes for cats. These resources are listed in the Appendix, and you are strongly encouraged to read what they have written. This recipe is the result of experimenting and using judgment about what cats need based on the scientific findings reported by those researchers, the example of commercial raw cat food producers, and personal experience of the author.

A. Cat Food Recipe for Option 3: Homemade

The basic recipe for raw cat food follows; each of the components will be discussed in turn. This recipe can be multiplied as many times as desired.

INGREDIENTS:
2½ pounds raw meaty bones and meat *or* 1½ pounds raw meat with calcium supplement
½ pound raw heart *or* 2000 mg Taurine
4 ounces raw liver *or* 3 ounces raw liver and 1 ounce raw kidney, sweetbreads, or other organ meat
3 ounces pulverized vegetables
8 ounces water
2 raw eggs *or* egg yolks
1 teaspoon fish body oil *or* salmon oil (**not** cod liver oil)
2 teaspoons kelp
1 teaspoon dulse, spirulina, or other seaweed; *or* 1 teaspoon barley grass, wheat grass, or other green grass
300 IU vitamin E
50 mg vitamin B complex
Optional: 2 capsules glandular supplement
Probiotics
Digestive Enzymes

EQUIPMENT:
Large pot or bowl to combine ingredients
Long wooden or metal spoon for mixing
Measuring spoons
Blender, food processor, juicer, or Vitamix® for pulverizing vegetables (and organ meats if you wish)
Sharp meat cleaver, butcher's knife, or Chinese cleaver (if cutting meat for grinding)
Meat grinder (if grinding bones and/or meat)
Small freezer containers

Although this basic recipe is straightforward, you must make some decisions along the way. The alternatives listed are not intended to make this difficult; rather, they are intended to show you how you can introduce variety into your cat's diet. To do so you can vary the types of meat used, the composition of the organs used, the types of vegetables included, the sources of minerals used, whether to grind bone or to use calcium supplement, and even sources of supplements.

There are two options for making this basic recipe, depending on how involved you want to get. The best option is to use ground raw meaty bones and meat as the meat source above. However, that is not always feasible for everyone. Therefore, a second best option is to use ground meat without bone and add a calcium supplement. These two options are described separately below.

Best Option: *Use 2½ pounds of ground raw meaty bones and meat*

The first step in preparing this recipe is to assemble the ingredients, starting with the animal products. Based on the proportion guidelines, grind or have ground meat that is roughly one half bone and one half muscle meat.[7] If you can find a butcher who will grind the bone and meat together, that is wonderful, especially if their equipment can grind beef, lamb, veal, or pork bones in addition to poultry bones. If you can not find a butcher who will grind bones for you, you can purchase an inexpensive meat grinder and grind your own. In the latter event, you will probably only be able to grind chicken bones and bones of other small poultry because of the limitations of home grinders.[8]

This process is much easier than it sounds. The key is becoming familiar with what constitutes a raw meaty bone and the desired proportions. The Ingredient Guide in Section 3 provides a comprehensive list to help you identify raw meaty bones.

If you have found a butcher who will grind bones for you, ask him to grind two and a half pounds of meat products so that one-half of the ground product is made up of ground bone. Realize that bone not only contains minerals but also contains other essential building blocks that contribute to your cat's health, particularly fat. Feeding too much bone typically leads to constipation, so you will want to observe your cat's elimination behavior at first to adjust the composition of the home made food to your cat's needs.

If you are grinding meat and bones yourself, it is assumed here that you will only be able to grind chicken and other small poultry bones. The easiest way to do this is to start with a whole chicken—choose a medium sized chicken that weighs between three and four pounds. Remove most of the skin and big pieces of fat. Cut off enough of the breast and thigh meat (and leg meat, if necessary) to leave a meaty carcass that weighs about two and a half pounds and is roughly 50% bone and 50% meat. Using a meat cleaver, Chinese cleaver, or butcher's knife, chop the carcass into pieces small enough to put through the meat grinder (you may want to chop through the larger pieces of bone, especially in the legs, wings, and back, just to make it a little easier on your grinder.) Put these pieces through the grinder.

You will also be grinding or chopping the organ meat. As noted above, raw heart is important to include because it contains significant amounts of the essential amino acid taurine. If you can not locate a source of raw heart, you must substitute 2000 mg taurine supplement. Raw liver provides a great deal of vitamins A and D as well as other important nutrients, and should comprise at least three quarters of the organ meat you use aside from the heart.[9] Since variety is important, you can include other organs, such as kidneys and sweetbreads, depending on availability and your cat's preferences.[10]

If you have found a good butcher, you can ask him to grind the heart, liver, and any other organs into the bone and meat, making your job easier. If you are grinding your own meat, you can put the heart, liver, and other organ meat through the grinder very easily. Alternatively, you can chop the organ meat finely or put it in a blender or food processor and add it to the other animal components so that the organs are distributed throughout the mix. Whichever option you choose, make sure to use the ground animal products quickly to retain freshness.

Once you have the ground meat, bones, and organs, you are almost ready to prepare the cat food recipe. First, however, you will need to assemble the other ingredients, including the pulverized vegetables. Vegetables need to be pulverized so that your cat's digestive system can access any nutrients and fiber they need. Without pulverizing, the hard cell walls in vegetable matter are impenetrable by the cat's digestive system, so they will just pass through without being digested.

To pulverize the vegetables, put an assortment through the grinder after you have ground the meat, bone, and organs—this will make clean-up easier, but this only is effective if you are using a small grinding die (otherwise, your cat may pick out the meat and leave the vegetables.) Alternatively, use your blender, food processor, juicer, or Vitamix® with a little water as needed to liquefy them. If you use a juicer, be sure to mix the pulp and juice together (don't throw away the pulp.) See the Ingredient Guide at the end of this chapter to determine what vegetables to use. Freeze unused vegetables in an ice cube tray and store in a plastic bag for future use.

If your cat simply refuses to eat vegetables, you do have an alternative. Eliminate vegetables and add 2 teaspoons of psyllium husk. Some researchers believe that cats do not extract any nutrients at all from the vegetables obtained in the digestive tracts of their prey.[11] Instead, they believe that the vegetable matter simple serves as indigestible fiber that helps keep the digestive tract working properly.

Even if this is true, since a cat's prey would contain semi-digested vegetation, not psyllium husk, a more natural approach is to include pulverized vegetables. Therefore, using psyllium husk is *not* recommended on a regular basis. However, as a last resort, if your cat rejects vegetables completely, substituting psyllium husk will offer similar gut clearing properties. If you do adopt this alternative, be sure that your cat is getting enough water in his food, since psyllium absorbs a lot of water and will cause constipation if too little water is ingested. The recipe includes sufficient water to account for this action of the psyllium.

All that remains before you can assemble the cat food is to gather together the other ingredients. Each warrants a word or two so that you are completely sure of what is intended:

- Water: use the best quality of water you can afford—as with people, water is an essential element in the cat's diet. Try to use water free from impurities and added chemicals, such as filtered or spring water.
- Raw eggs: simply crack eggs into the bone, meat, organ, and vegetable mixture, or include only the egg yolks and save the whites for your cooking.[12]

- Fish body or salmon oil: These oils supplement your cat's diet with Omega-3 fatty acids, which are very important for healthy skin, coat, and proper functioning of other metabolic systems. It is especially important to include these if your meat sources are not high in Omega-3s. You may be able to find poultry and eggs that are high in Omega-3s because the chickens have been fed flax seed in their diets, but in general, most conventional meat sources do not provide sufficient quantities. Although some vegetable oils, such as flax seed oil (or ground flax seed), primrose oil, and borage oil, are good sources of Omega-3s for humans, cats appear to do better with animal sources. These oils are very sensitive to heat and can become rancid easily. Choose sources that are kept refrigerated or are impervious to air, such as gel caps. Keep oils refrigerated to preserve freshness.
- Kelp: This is one of the best sources of important vitamins and trace minerals that are essential to many biological functions. The less processed the kelp is, the better. Cats generally like it because it has a fishy taste and aroma.
- Dulse, spirulina, or other seaweed; barley grass, wheat grass, or other green grass: all of these additional supplements provide different combinations of vitamins and minerals. In the interest of providing ample variety for your cat, buy small quantities of each in as whole forms as possible. Don't worry if you can't find them all; they are merely suggestions to help you consider your options to create variety.
- Vitamin E: this vitamin is typically sold in liquid, in gel caps, or in dry form, usually in 100 or 400 IU dosages. The easiest way to add vitamin E to this recipe is to buy liquid vitamin E in a bottle with a dropper. Buy from a good quality human grade source.
- Vitamin B complex: purchase 50 mg pills or capsules. Capsules are easier to use than pills—simply open them into the mixture. Otherwise, crush pills using a mortar and pestle or pill crusher.
- Probiotics[13]: these are lactobacillus, acidophilus and other good bacteria that populate the cat's intestines; feeding them helps promote absorption of nutrients. Human probiotics are typically less expensive than those designed for animals, but have the drawback that it is more difficult to determine quantity. For using human probiotics in this recipe, include

one human dosage based on package directions; if you buy probiotics made specifically for dogs and cats, follow directions for amount per three pounds of food.
- Digestive enzymes: these are enzymes that help to break down food. They are particularly important when first making the switch to raw and for animals as they age: in both cases, adding enzymes helps to break down the food in the stomach so that nutrients can be absorbed more readily. Some cats may need a little help breaking down raw meat and bone initially; they tend to stop needing them after their systems adapt to digesting the raw food. Some older animals may continue to need them to get the most from their diet.

Once you have the ground bone and meat, organs, and vegetables together, and have assembled all the other ingredients, you are almost finished. Add the water, eggs, kelp and other seaweed or grasses, vitamins E and B complex, fish body or salmon oil, and probiotics to the bone, meat, organs, and vegetables. Also add the digestive enzymes and glandular supplement[14], if desired. Stir the mixture as little as possible to incorporate all the ingredients; if you mix too much, the mixture becomes gummy and pasty. Once all ingredients are combined, portion them into small containers that are sufficient for one or two meals and put them in the freezer.

Second Best Option: *Use ground meat and add calcium supplement*

Finding a butcher willing to grind meat and bones for you is difficult these days; buying a meat grinder and doing it yourself takes time and effort, and you must exercise patience so as not to break the grinder. They are worth doing because providing your cat with raw meaty bones is the best possible source of the essential building blocks for optimal health. However, these options are not necessarily possible or suitable for everyone.

A second best alternative to using ground raw bone in the basic recipe is to use ground meat and add calcium supplement. You can purchase ground meat easily from grocery stores or grind it yourself in a food processor or meat grinding attachment to some mixers. This option makes it simple to introduce variety, because you will find both whole and ground beef, lamb, pork, chicken, and turkey widely available in your grocery store.[15]

In order to ensure that your cat gets the calcium he needs to sustain health, you will need to add a calcium supplement that is appropriate to the raw diet. Raw meat itself has significant amounts of phosphorous and very little calcium. The skeletal system of your cat, as well as many other systems, depends on a proper ratio of calcium to phosphorous. Without sufficient calcium added to raw meat, your cat will not have enough calcium to balance the high phosphorous content and will suffer ill effects eventually. Be aware that there are calcium supplements sold for cats and dogs that have only small amounts of calcium and tend to include phosphorous, vitamin D, and other ingredients—these are NOT what you want to add to the raw diet. Rather, you want a pure calcium supplement to add to the raw meat.

It is recommended that you use a natural calcium source that has not been cooked. Bone meal, which is frequently used as a calcium supplement in home made cat food, has been cooked, and in some cases bone meal has been found to contain high quantities of lead. While it can be used, other sources are preferable. Unfortunately, alternative sources are difficult to find. The most likely sources are ground raw bones and a natural calcium supplement made from seaweed.[16] To find a natural, uncooked calcium source, refer to the resource guide in the Appendix or consult your veterinarian.

Once you have obtained the ground meat and the calcium supplement, everything else is the same as in previous case: finely chop or blend the heart, liver, and any other organ meat you are using; pulverize the vegetables; then combine all the remaining ingredients and parcel into small containers for the freezer. That's all there is to it.

B. Preparing the Alternate Raw Meaty Bone and Meat Meals for Option 2: Commercial plus RMB and for Option 3b: Homemade plus RMB

Preparing the meals to alternate with the commercial or home made raw cat food is a simple process. These meals are intended to give your cat the opportunity to chew raw meaty bones and raw muscle meat. The action of chewing helps to clean their teeth, exercise their whole body, and satisfy an instinct for chewing that helps them emotionally.

Whether you feed the commercial or home made raw cat food, follow the same principles: feed two meals per day; at one meal, feed the ground food, and at the other meal, feed the whole food (whether you feed the ground food morning or evening is entirely up to you.) Feed a meal of raw meaty bones for the alternate meal one day; the next day, feed a meal of raw muscle meat.

Here is an example in which a person feeds the ground food in the morning:

Day 1—morning:	feed ground raw food (commercial or home made)
Day 1—evening:	feed raw meaty bones
Day 2—morning:	feed ground raw food
Day 2—evening:	feed raw meat

Repeat this pattern over and over again and you will easily be providing your cat with a diet that reflects the ideal proportions listed in the Ingredient Guide at the end of this chapter.

All you need to do to feed this way is to purchase the raw meaty bones and meat, parcel them into meal sized amounts, and depending on your cat's preferences, cut them into chewable pieces. Pieces should be big enough that your cat needs to chew and will not just swallow the piece whole. Some cats will eat larger pieces of raw meaty bone and meat than others. You will have to gauge your cat's preferences by observing what he will eat. If you find he will not eat the raw meaty bones, try cutting them into smaller pieces.

Poultry shears are particularly useful in cutting raw meaty bones into small pieces. A Chinese cleaver is also a great tool for chopping raw meaty bones into small pieces. Alternatively, place raw meaty bones under a towel and hit them with a hammer to break up the bone, then cut through the meat and bone with a knife. Your cat will still need to chew, but will not be daunted by big pieces of bone.

You will need a couple of important pieces of equipment: one is a sharp knife, meat cleaver, Chinese cleaver, or poultry shears to cut up the pieces of raw meaty bones or meat; the other is a kitchen scale to measure out the amount desired. Initially, it will take more effort to measure the right amount, but over time, you will be able to estimate the right amount easily. Simply place the small pieces in your cat's bowl and watch him become the carnivore you know him to be!

C. Implementing Option 4: RMB Rotation

Option 4 is, paradoxically, the most challenging to conceptualize but the easiest to implement. The reason for this is that it takes more forethought and attention so that you ensure you are providing balance and variety over time, but it requires much less work on the part of the feeder because the cat does more of the work by chewing.

The premise of Option 4 is that you feed all the same ingredients that are put into the homemade raw cat food, but you just don't take the time and effort to grind everything and mix it together. You will still have to pulverize vegetables, but everything else can be offered to the cat in chewable pieces. The trick is to offer these components on a rotating basis so that, over time, your cat is eating all the components of a healthful raw diet.

It is recommended that you become familiar with the ingredients of the homemade ground food before you attempt to use Option 4. Once you are comfortable with the composition of the homemade food and the proportions of those ingredients in the diet, you will then be better able to feed the components separately.

One caveat is that feeding this option requires the cooperation of your cat to eat everything you feed: if your cat routinely refuses an important component, such as the organ meat or the vegetables, then you may be best off reverting to Option 2 or Option 3b.

The easiest way to appreciate this feeding option is to consider an example of a typical feeding plan for a two week period. Table 2 displays a two week feeding schedule that incorporates all of the ingredients in the raw diet in the right proportions by feeding two meals based on raw meaty bones and then one meal based on raw meat. This is just one possible way to feed, which can be modified to suit your needs and your cat's preferences.

To entice cats to eat vegetables, vitamins, and other supplements that might be rejected, they are added to the meat meals and frequently combined with enticing elements like liver, heart, and kidney. Remember that variety is introduced by feeding different types of raw meaty bones, raw meat, organs, vegetables, and to a lesser extent, other seaweeds and grasses.

Following a feeding plan such as this is relatively simple: at each meal, all you have to do is cut up the raw meaty bones or meat (and organ meat, if being fed) and, if appropriate, add the one or two other elements. As you can see, all the elements of the home made food are provided over the course of two weeks, although not at every meal. Moreover, by feeding this way, you achieve the ideal proportions listed in the Ingredient Guide. In this way, balance is achieved over time and your cat will receive the optimal nutrition you can provide.

EXAMPLE OF A TWO WEEK FEEDING SCHEDULE
FOR OPTION 4: RMB Rotation

DAY	MORNING MEAL	EVENING MEAL
1	Raw meaty bones cut into chewable pieces (add enzymes to meals as needed)	Raw meat pieces and 1-2 teaspoons raw liver cut up with ¼-½ tsp. pulverized vegetables stirred in and probiotics added
2	Raw meaty bones cut into chewable pieces	Raw meaty bones cut into chewable pieces

3	Raw meat pieces with vitamins and 1-2 ounces raw heart cut up	Raw meaty bones cut into chewable pieces
4	Raw meaty bones cut into chewable pieces	Raw meat pieces with 3-4 drops salmon oil and 1/8 tsp. kelp (a "pinch")
5	Raw meaty bones cut into chewable pieces	Raw meaty bones cut into chewable pieces
6	Raw meat pieces with 1-2 tsp. raw egg yolk	Raw meaty bones cut into chewable pieces
7	Raw meaty bones cut into chewable pieces	Raw meat pieces with 1-2 teaspoons raw liver cut up with ¼-½ tsp. pulverized vegetables stirred in
8	Raw meaty bones cut into chewable pieces	Raw meaty bones cut into chewable pieces
9	Raw meat pieces with vitamins and 1-2 ounces raw kidney cut up and probiotics added	Raw meaty bones cut into chewable pieces
10	Raw meaty bones cut into chewable pieces	Raw meat pieces with 1-2 tsp. raw egg yolk and ¼-½ tsp. pulverized vegetables stirred in
11	Raw meaty bones cut into chewable pieces	Raw meaty bones cut into chewable pieces
12	Raw meat pieces with 3-4 drops salmon oil and vitamins	Raw meaty bones cut into chewable pieces
13	Raw meaty bones cut into chewable pieces	Raw meat pieces and 1/8 tsp. dulse added (a "pinch")
14	Raw meaty bones cut into chewable pieces	Raw meaty bones cut into chewable pieces

Cutting RMB into chewable pieces and pulverizing vegetables will result in something that looks as follows:

A few additional items need to be noted with regard to Option 4. First, vegetables often pose a problem for raw feeders. Remember that cats are carnivores and that vegetables should comprise a very small proportion of the total diet (in general, no more than 10% of the total diet.) If your cat is rejecting meals with vegetables, odds are you are adding too much or including pungent ingredients that are off-putting to your cat. See the Ingredient Guide for more details about vegetable types to include.

Cats are more likely to eat the vegetables if they are combined with food they really like, so including vegetables with meat meals, in meals that have organ meat in them, or along with salmon oil may prove easier for you both. Cutting meat pieces small and coating them with the pulverized vegetables so that your cat pays less attention to them also helps.

Other options exist for coaxing your cat to eat meals with vegetables or other ingredients he doesn't like. One option is to add between a half teaspoon and a teaspoon of room temperature, no salt chicken or beef stock. A convenient way to do this is to pour stock into ice cube trays and freeze, then pull out one cube at a time to defrost. Another option is to sprinkle the food with dried fish flakes, such as bonito or crumbled freeze dried salmon. Not every solution will work for every cat, so you will have to experiment to determine what works.

Canned tuna, salmon, or mackerel are sometimes useful additions to coax a reluctant cat to eat. It is recommended, however, that you *not* use canned fish on a regular basis. If you do so regularly, odds are your cat will come to expect it at every meal and may become "addicted" to it. Canned fish is cooked and often contains a lot of salt—although it is fine to give canned fish as an occasional treat—or as a fall back in the event that you forget to defrost something for dinner!—it is *not* recommended as an integral part of the raw diet. (I call canned tuna "pizza for cats".)

In the event that your cat absolutely refuses to eat vegetables, there is one other option that you can resort to using: psyllium husk. As mentioned before, this is not the preferred option. However, after all other options have been exhausted, psyllium husk can be added to a cat's food in place of vegetables. Your cat will not have access to any nutritive value that vegetables might have imparted, but psyllium husk will provides the indigestible fiber needed to cleanse the intestine and promote gut motility.

If your cat simply refuses to eat vegetables of any type, you can try this alternative by sprinkling a pinch of psyllium husk (between and eighth and a quarter of a teaspoon) onto food in place of vegetables, then add between a half and a full teaspoon of water and let the psyllium soak up the water before feeding. It is important to add water to food with psyllium because it will absorb a lot of moisture as it moves through the cat's digestive tract and could cause constipation if too much is added without sufficient water.

Vitamins also present a challenge in feeding cats using Option 4. Unlike other options, vitamins tend to be bitter and are less easily disguised by being mixed into other ingredients. It is worth considering why we add vitamins to the cat's food in the first place to help determine your best option for using them.

In theory, the raw food diet contains all the vitamins, minerals, and other building blocks for your cat's proper nutrition. Unlike processed, cooked cat food—which requires that vitamins and minerals be added back after having destroyed the naturally occurring ones through the heating process—raw food theoretically contains everything the body needs to be healthy.

Hence, adding vitamin supplements to your cat's food is not critical. Nevertheless, it is recommended that you consider adding them occasionally for the same reason that people take vitamins: we simply don't know whether the food that is currently available to us through modern production technologies provides us with sufficient quantities of all the nutrients we need to support health. Therefore, it is up to you whether you want to add vitamin supplements to your cat's diet. In general, it is a good idea to add vitamins B complex and vitamin E two to three times a week.

If you choose to add vitamins to your cat's food, you have some options. First, you can add individual vitamins separately. Following the ingredients in the recipe, you can limit your supplements to vitamin B complex and vitamin E. However, the bitterness of these vitamins may result in your cat refusing to eat. Another option is to purchase prepared vitamin supplements from your veterinarian or another reliable source. These vitamin supplements will have much more in them than only these two vitamins, so if you choose to use them, you only want to feed them occasionally, as is the case in the biweekly feeding plan.

If you purchase vitamin complex supplements, be sure they are suitable for a raw diet. Many vitamin supplements on the market are intended to be used to supplement dry cat food, which already has substantial vitamins added back to it. These products typically have such small amounts of vitamins that they are not appropriate for raw diets. Some suggestions for vitamins are listed in the resource section in the Appendix. You may also want to consult your veterinarian for vitamins, enzymes, and probiotics that they have experience with and recommend given your cat's particular needs.

4. The Feeding Process

Once you have decided which option to choose, the feeding process is very straightforward. First, determine the amount to begin feeding each day and then divide that amount into two meals. Next, prepare meal-sized packages to put in the freezer or refrigerator ready to be warmed for eating. Serve ground food directly; for raw meaty bone or meat meals, cut into pieces, add ingredients if feeding Option 4: RMB Rotation, and serve.

A. Amounts to Feed

Determining the amount to feed your cat is more of an art than a science. As with people, every cat is different: each has different metabolism and different levels of activity that will warrant either more or less food. In general, younger and more active cats will require more food, older and less active cats will require less food.

Typically, you will feed your cat between three and five percent of his ideal body weight each day. To calculate the amount of food you will feed, use the following formula:

(a) (Ideal body weight in pounds) x (16 ounces/pound) x (percent of body weight) = Ounces of food to feed per day

(b) Ounces of food to feed per meal = Ounces of food to feed per day / 2

Table 3 below provides you with a quick reference for determining how much to feed based on your cat's ideal body weight.

Table 3: Typical Amounts to Feed Per Meal

	Percent of Body Weight	
Ideal Weight	3%	5%
7 pounds	7 lb. x (16 oz./lb.) x 3% = 3.36 oz. Divided into 2 meals per day = **1.7 oz. per meal**	7 lb. x (16 oz./lb.) x 5% = 5.6 oz. Divided into 2 meals per day = **2.8 oz. per meal**
10 pounds	10 lb. x (16 oz./lb.) x 3% = 4.8 oz. Divided into 2 meals per day = **2.4 oz. per meal**	10 lb. x (16 oz./lb.) x 5% = 8 oz. Divided into 2 meals per day = **4 oz. per meal**
12 pounds	12 lb. x (16 oz./lb.) x 3% = 5.8 oz. Divided into 2 meals per day = **2.9 oz. per meal**	12 lb. x (16 oz./lb.) x 5% = 9.6 oz. Divided into 2 meals per day = **4.8 oz. per meal**
15 pounds	15 lb. x (16 oz./lb.) x 3% = 7.2 oz. Divided into 2 meals per day = **3.6 oz. per meal**	15 lb. x (16 oz./lb.) x 5% = 12 oz. Divided into 2 meals per day = **6 oz. per meal**
20 pounds	20 lb. x (16 oz./lb.) x 3% = 9.6oz. Divided into 2 meals per day = **4.8 oz. per meal**	20 lb. x (16 oz./lb.) x 5% = 16 oz. Divided into 2 meals per day = **8 oz. per meal**
NOTE: These amounts are average amounts to achieve over time—if one meal is a little more, make the next meal a little less		

That means that a cat whose ideal weight is 12 pounds will eat two meals per day that are between 2.9 and 4.8 ounces, depending on metabolism and activity level. The best approach when you first begin feeding a raw diet is to start at the lower percentage and increase amounts if your cat begins to lose weight. So for a 12 pound cat, begin by feeding just under 3 ounces of food per meal. If your cat starts to lose weight, increase the quantity of food slowly, paying close attention to his body weight. If he starts to gain too much weight, reduce the quantity a bit. Keep in mind that these measurements are approximate starting places, so you do not need to worry too much if one meal is slightly over or under the intended quantity. Once again, balance over time is the goals, so aim for these quantities over time, observe closely, and adjust as your cat dictates.

B. Adapting the System for Kittens

This system can easily be adapted for feeding kittens after they have been weaned. The most significant differences are (i) that you will feed kittens 7 to 10% of body weight per day, and (ii) that you will initially feed very small meals, dividing daily rations into four meals, then gradually decreasing to three meals a day, until finally backing down to two meals a day. Typically, four meals a day are fed between weaning at approximately 8 weeks old to 12 weeks. As kittens get bigger, decrease to three meals per day from 12 weeks to 20 weeks. At about 20 weeks, you should be able to adjust to two meals per day.

Calculate the feeding amount the same way as for adult cats, based on current body weight and the desired percent of weight, then divide by the number of meals. Growing kittens will need a higher percentage of body weight to sustain growth, so start at 8% of body weight and then back down as the kitten gets bigger.

Growing cats need a lot of protein and bone to help them develop healthy skeletal and immune systems. Use raw meaty bones that are close to 2/3 bone in feeding. It is valuable to offer unground bones to kittens early so they will become used to chewing them. Try introducing unground bones around the time you switch from four meals per day to three per day. Just be sure that the pieces are cut small enough for your kitten to get his mouth around but not so small that they can be swallowed whole.

Especially with kittens, keep track of what you feed and what his reactions are. Feeding digestive enzymes when switching to raw is always a good idea, and it is particularly so as kittens begin to mature. It is an especially good idea to work with a veterinarian who supports raw feeding and who can recommend other supplements to help support your young cat's needs as he develops. In the end, you will have a very strong, healthy cat who will have had the best food available his whole life.

C. Making the System Work

Once you have decided on the feeding option to use on a regular basis and have determined the quantity to begin feeding, you are ready to feed the raw diet. The easiest way to do this is to take a little time to prepare meal-sized packages and freeze them so that you will not have to do much work any other time. Take packages out of the freezer as needed: an easy way to be sure that you remember to defrost the next meal is to remove it from the freezer immediately after feeding the previous meal. For example, after feeding breakfast, take dinner out of the freezer and leave it on the counter or in the refrigerator to defrost. Bacteria is not a great concern because of the cat's acidic stomach; freshness is more critical to entice the cat to eat. If the food warms up too quickly, simply put it in the refrigerator until meal time. Alternatively, allow to defrost in the refrigerator a day before needed. Rest assured that after an initial adjustment period when you are developing a pattern, feeding this way will be as natural as feeding processed food used to be.

5. Making the Switch

Switching from processed food to raw food can be unnerving for you, but you need not be concerned about your cat. Cat's are naturally creatures of habit, so initially, your cat is likely to resist the change. He will learn very quickly, however, that you are offering him food that is preferable to what he has had before. The most important element to making a successful switch is patience. Start slow, let your cat adjust to the change, and wait for him to realize that raw food is really better food.

A. Going Cold Turkey

The best way to make the switch to raw food is to stop feeding all processed food at once. This approach is somewhat different than what is often recommended when changing an animal's feed. There are a couple of reasons why the cold turkey approach is preferable to a gradual switch. First, the cat's body digests grains more quickly than meat and bone, so if you combine them, odds are the body will not adapt to digesting the raw meat and bone as quickly and easily.

Second, cats are typically "addicted" to the food they have been eating; if you combine what they know with what they don't know, they will simply wait for you to give them what they know, picking out the part they like and even skipping a meal, if necessary.

Finally, eliminating processed food completely from the diet means eliminating ingredients that are or produce toxins in the body; the sooner he stops ingesting them, the healthier your cat will become.

So how do you make the switch? With a simple introduction of raw meat, gradually introducing bone, and eventually, all the other components of the raw diet. The switch to raw *should* be gradual, in that the amount of food that you feed should initially be small and should be increased gradually to allow your cat's system to adjust.

Starting slowly is the best way to ensure that your cat responds well to his new diet. Throughout the switch, you will want to observe your cat carefully, so you may want to arrange to start on a weekend or during a time period when you will be around to take account of his behavior.

Regardless of the feeding option you choose, start by skipping one meal. This will not hurt your cat; what it will do is give his system a chance to clear out the remnants of the processed food that are still in it, and will leave him hungry so that he will be more interested in the new food.

Begin by feeding a meal that is one third of the amount you are aiming to feed on a regular basis. As you begin to feed raw meat and bones, add a digestive enzyme made for cats and dogs. This will give his system a little help as it reverts to it's natural way of digesting raw meat and bones. Digestive Enzyme sources are listed in the Appendix and may be available from your veterinarian; you can feed these for the first month or until you feel your cat has completely adapted to the new diet, and any time you see any changes in his digestion.

Observe your cat closely after he eats and throughout the day. You will be watching primarily for vomiting and diarrhea, both of which may occur the first time you feed. Most cats will experience neither, but do not be alarmed if this happens. Your cat's system may be reacting to the new food because it is foreign. In addition, your cat's body is eliminating toxins that have built up over time. This cleansing process is a good thing that only lasts a day or so. It is important to observe your cat because these conditions should not linger—if your cat either vomits or has diarrhea for more than two days, you should seek professional help from a veterinarian or other specialist experienced in feeding the raw diet. Keep in mind that this occurrence is extremely rare.

Feed the one-third ration for the first two meals. If your cat is fine, then increase the amount to two-thirds of the amount you are aiming for and continue to observe. Do this for meals three through six (days 2 and 3). If your cat is fine at this point, then increase to the full ration. Otherwise, keep him on two-thirds ration for another day and continue to observe. He should be ready to move to the full amount by the fifth day.

If you are feeding Option 1, or Option 3a, you will simply be introducing the ground food gradually. If you are feeding Option 2 or Option 3b, begin introducing alternate meals immediately in small amounts: feed one-third the amount of ground food at the first meal; at the second meal, feed one-third the amount of raw meat. The next day, feed two thirds of the ground food at one meal and two thirds of raw meaty bones at the next meal. This way, your cat will become accustomed to the pattern as he adapts to the new food.

If you are feeding Option 4, begin with one-third of the amount of raw meat alone at each meal for the first day. On the second day, give one third the amount or raw meaty bones at one meal, and two thirds the amount of raw meat in the other. Repeat this pattern the next day. Finally, on the fourth day, if things are progressing normally, begin feeding the full amount. Go more slowly if your cat seems to warrant it.

B. Dealing with Refusals to Eat

Being a cat, yours may refuse to make the change because he is not used to what you are offering. He is accustomed to food that has had ingredients added to it to make it palatable and aromatically appealing to cats. You can do the same thing to entice your cat to eat the food that you know is better for him.

The first issue to address is to be sure that the food is room temperature or warmer. Cats prefer food that is not cold, which makes sense, since most cats will eat their prey immediately after killing it. The best way to ensure that the food is room temperature is to leave it to defrost on the kitchen counter during the day or overnight. If the food is still cold at meal time, place it wrapped in plastic or foil into a bowl of hot water for five minutes.

Do not put raw food in the microwave or heat it on the stove, as the heating process will change the molecular structure of the food. This will be particularly problematic for the bone, and will make digestion of it very difficult if not impossible. However, in making the transition, some people find it useful to sear the outside of the meat in order to create an appetizing aroma. Obviously, this is only feasible for feeding raw meat meals, but can be an option to use during the initial switch. Gradually wean your cat off the seared meat to fully raw meat over the course of the first week.

Another option to warm the cat's food as well as to create a meat-scented aroma is to add warmed chicken, beef, or other meat stock to your cat's food. Simply warm a tablespoon or two of stock and add a little to the food. Odds are, your cat will try it because it smells good.

Another option is to add dried fish flakes. Nearly all cats are tempted by the odor of fish, so he is more likely to be interested if he smells it in this new food. Dried fish flakes are sometimes available in pet stores and can often be found in Asian food stores or in grocery stores where Asian food is sold. See the appendix for some sources of fish flakes. You can also try using the juice from canned fish such as tuna, mackerel, or salmon. This tends to work extremely well, but has the drawback that cats start to demand it. Be careful not to make this a habit.

You should be able to coax your cat to try the new food by using these techniques combined with hunger. If he is still refusing to eat, you may need to try an alternative feeding option. For example, if you are trying to feed Option 2, you have a couple of alternatives: one is to find a different brand of commercial food that he may prefer; another is to make your own food and follow Option 3b instead; or to dive into Option 4. If he is rejecting your homemade food, you may be including too many vegetables or using a kind of meat he doesn't like or that is not fresh enough for him. Keep it simple and let him guide you about what you can and can not do. In the event your cat simply will not eat, do not let him starve—go back to feeding the processed food and locate a veterinarian or other specialist with experience in feeding a raw diet to cats and try again with their help.

Section 2 provided you with everything you need to know in order to feed your cat a healthful raw diet. A few additional items should be mentioned to help you implement this regimen as practically and conveniently as possible.

6. Keeping Track of Your Practices and Progress

One of the most important things that you can do, especially at the beginning, is keep track of what you are doing. It is recommended that you start a notebook to keep track of what you are feeding and to note your cat's reactions, both good and bad. Particularly for the first three months, it is recommended that you note what you fed at each meal, including supplements, so that you can identify any particular food or supplement that doesn't agree with your cat. You will also be able to distinguish those things he likes from those he dislikes. Finally, you will be able to keep track of what he is eating to make sure that he is getting the right balance of nutrients over time. This will be especially important if you are making the food yourself under Options 3 or 4. You will be able to demonstrate to your vet exactly what you are feeding. Moreover, this will give you confidence to try new things that you might not feel comfortable exploring otherwise.

Before starting, it is also a good idea to create a "before" file—that is, a file that includes pictures of your cat and your description of his physical condition before you begin the raw diet. Include descriptions of his weight, the condition of his coat, skin, teeth, eyes, and any medical conditions he has, his activity and energy levels, his attitudes and sociability, his eating patterns, the state of his stool, and anything else that you can think of about him. Include a "before" picture so that you can tell what happens to his fur and teeth as a result of the switch. This will become very useful later because you will inevitably observe changes in your cat's physical and emotional well being. By cataloguing his qualities "before", you will be able to compare them more easily "after".

7. Finding and Choosing Meat Sources

Meat and bones will be the primary source of food for your cat, so identifying the best sources you can afford will be very important. The options range from purchasing meat from organically fed, pasture raised animals to buying the cheapest cuts from your local grocery store.

The advantage of pasture raised meat is that it will not have hormones, steroids, antibiotics, and other residues that are present in conventionally-raised meat. The disadvantages are that such meat is quite a bit more costly and may involve more time and energy to locate and purchase, because many sellers only sell whole or half animals, meaning that you will have to do more work to prepare meals.

Grocery store meats are very convenient and tend to be most affordable. However, they typically come from animals that have been fed less natural diets and have been given drugs to keep them healthy and manage their growth. As a result, the meat tends to contain additives that may or may not be a problem for your cat. It is also worth noting that conventionally farmed animals are considered by some people to be raised using methods that are unpalatable or inhumane.

Conventionally produced meats also have the disadvantage of having been processed quite a bit before being sold to you. Chickens, in particular, have gone through a lot of processing and so will not be quite as fresh as chicken available from a source closer to the farm. Some cats are pickier than others about the freshness of their meat. In addition, it is often difficult to find bones available in grocery stores any more. You may be able to make special arrangements with the butcher to get chicken backs, necks, and other small bones in bulk quantities. Another option is to investigate wholesale meat markets and make deals to purchase scraps and carcasses at a discount.

Other options also exist for getting a variety of meat and bones. Ethnic grocery stores sometimes have varieties of meat that are not available in conventional U.S. grocery stores. Halal and Kosher meat markets often have meat available that is fresher and with fewer additives than available conventionally. Finding farms in your area that sell pasture raised chicken, beef, lamb, etc., are worth investigating to see whether you can make a deal for large quantities and then store at home.

No matter what you decide is right for you, your cat will be better off than if he were eating processed food. Use your judgment about what you can afford, how much time you want to take purchasing food and preparing meals, and how much capacity you have to freeze meat and bones. Again, start simply and increase in complexity as you grow in knowledge, confidence, and comfort about feeding this diet.

8. Fears and Concerns

It is entirely understandable that this approach to feeding cats may generate some fears and concerns for you. After all, this is contrary to the conventional wisdom that most of us have been exposed to our whole lives. Most conventional veterinarians do not support a raw diet because they have not been taught anything about it in vet school, where the little bit of nutritional education they receive typically comes from pet food manufacturers. Some well intentioned veterinarians blame raw feeding for producing physical problems that are unrelated to the diet because it is an easy scapegoat, since they are not familiar enough with its benefits.

You will need to be brave as you approach these well-meaning doctors, because they may contribute to your fears and concerns needlessly. Rest assured that you are making the right choice because you know your cat, and you know that he is better off physically and emotionally on this diet. Two issues of particular concern to many new raw feeders and veterinarians are issues concerning bones and bacteria.

A. Issues Concerning Feeding Bones

Many people worry about feeding bones because they have always heard that bones are dangerous. This book acknowledges that feeding cats *cooked* bone can be very dangerous.

Since cooked bones are hard, they shatter easily producing sharp edges that can and often do puncture internal organs of an animal who ingests them. Cooked bones that do not damage organs as they pass through the digestive tract can cause other problems. The heating process changes their molecular structure so the animal's digestive system can not break them down into absorbable components. Most veterinarians who oppose feeding raw meaty bones have horror stories to tell about bones being impacted in an animal's digestive tract and/or puncturing nearby organs.

Unlike cooked bone, raw bone is soft and appropriately sized pieces can be chewed and digested by cats. Most chicken bones, for example, can easily be cut with a sharp knife or pair of poultry shears. Cat's teeth are precisely intended to crunch and chew the soft bones of small mammals and birds. Moreover, the chemical composition of raw bone is such that a cat digests and absorbs protein, fat, vitamins, and minerals, breaking them down into their constituent parts that are the most natural building blocks for peak health. Problems are typically eliminated by avoiding large bones and long, weight bearing bones that tend to be harder than other parts of the skeleton.

Very little scientific, controlled research has been undertaken to study the benefits of feeding raw meat and bones to cats. Commercial pet food manufacturers have little, if anything, to gain from such studies, and much to lose. They typically are the ones who provide funding for education and research into animal nutrition and sometimes they even teach nutrition in veterinary schools. Fortunately, a few veterinarians and animal nutritionists are promoting inquiry into these questions about raw feeding, and hopefully, more scientific proof will be forthcoming shortly.

In the meantime, veterinarians and their clients who feed the raw diet have substantial amounts of anecdotal evidence to prove that feeding raw meaty bones and meat is the single most effective way to promote health in our feline family members. Most people who switch to raw experience no problems with animals eating raw bone.

However, there are always exceptions. An animal who gulps his food may swallow relatively large pieces that are not easily digested, leading to stomach upset, vomiting, and possible obstruction. An animal who is vomiting as a result of too large a piece of bone can be helped by giving soft food to help envelop the piece of bone that is stuck in the stomach and move it through the digestive tract more effectively. Raw feeders with "gulpers" will need to take appropriate action to feed large enough pieces so that the animal needs to chew well, or alternatively, exclusively feed home made or commercial ground food.

B. Bacteria and Parasites

One of the most common concerns among conventional vets and potential raw feeders is the question of bacteria and parasites. People mistakenly believe that bacteria, such as e. coli and salmonella, which can be deadly to humans, are also harmful to cats. This simply is not the case for the large majority of healthy cats.

Cats have a stomach environment that is significantly more acidic than that of humans. As a result, the acid kills the bacteria that would otherwise harm a human being. If you are concerned about bacteria on the surface of meat, you can soak raw meat in food grade hydrogen peroxide or grapefruit seed extract before feeding. Note that this is *food grade* hydrogen peroxide and grape*fruit* seed extract, not grape seed extract. Both should be available at health food stores. Although soaking in either of these agents can be done for peace of mind, neither is necessary unless your cat is seriously immune compromised. Be sure to rinse meat well after doing so; although neither will hurt your cat, neither has a very good taste.

Parasites are not necessarily killed in this environment. Therefore, it is very important that the food fed be free of parasites. Always feeding human grade meat is the best approach to avoid parasites. Trichinosis, a parasite that was frequently found in pork, is not as great a problem as it once was. The parasite arises when pigs are fed slops; in modern farming methods, most pigs are fed grains and other controlled ingredients, so trichinosis is rarely a problem. If you want to feed pork—which cats love—and are still worried, simply freeze the pork for at least two days—the freezing process will kill any parasite present. Therefore, unless your cat has an impaired immune system that would make him vulnerable to pathogens that are otherwise harmful, you need not worry about bacteria and parasites.

Since freshness is of paramount importance to cats, a good practice is to buy meat in as whole pieces as possible. Buying inexpensive cuts of beef rather than ground beef, and whole chickens rather than chicken parts, makes it more likely that your cat will find the meat fresh. Buying whole pieces reduces the amount of surface area on the meat that is exposed to the air and bacteria that can begin the spoilage process.

A bigger concern about handling raw meat has nothing to do with your cat, and everything to do with you and your family. As with any other meat handling, cleanliness is essential to avoid contamination to humans. Good meat handling practices include washing cutting boards, utensils, countertops, containers, and hands with soapy, very hot water to eliminate bacteria. Anti-bacterial soaps are not necessary to remove bacteria. Following good, conventional meat handling procedures and keeping raw meat away from small children or people with compromised immune systems are all that is needed to protect your family and yourself from contamination.

9. Conclusion

In this chapter, you have everything you need to know to provide raw food for your cat and to make the switch to raw food from a processed diet. If you are choosing Options 1 or 2, refer to the Appendix to find possible sources for commercially prepared raw food. You will probably need to make some phone calls or e-mails to locate a supplier. If you choose Options 2, 3a, 3b, or 4, use the Ingredient

Guide in Section 3 to determine what to include in your home made ground food and your alternate raw meaty bone and raw meat meals, as well as what vegetables and supplements to add to your cat's food. After a short adjustment period, both of you will have adapted to the new procedures and your cat will be convinced that you are feeding him great food.

Section 3

Ingredient Guide

1. Meat, Bones, and Vegetables

Identifying ingredients to include in your cats diet is quite simple. The only components in the raw diet are "raw meaty bones", raw muscle meat, organ meat, pulverized vegetables, eggs, and a few supplements. This *is* simple.

An easy way to see the big picture of the diet is to consider again the proportions that you are aiming for: 90% of the diet is meat based, 10% is vegetable based. Of the meat components, 60% is RMB, 30% is meat, and 10% are organs and eggs. These are intended to be guidelines, not hard and fast rules. Use your judgment about your cat's tastes and needs and adjust accordingly. They are meant to help guide, not lock you into a formula.

So what are some examples of these components?

+ **Raw Meaty Bones** (RMB) include: chicken backs, necks, breast frames, wings; lean part of rabbit, turkey necks, small fowl backs, necks, breast frames; neck bones and rib bones of beef, lamb, pork, veal, game (generally need to be ground by butcher). Some chicken RMB are pictured below:

+ **Raw Meat** includes: chicken leg, thigh, breast (with or without bone), Cornish game hen or other poultry breast, thigh, and leg, meatier parts of the rabbit, whole fish, shrimp with or without shells, stew meat, tongue, other flesh from any animal; only rarely, canned fish (mackerel, salmon, tuna—all packed in water, not oil, rinsed to remove salt if desired—cats can get addicted to these!) Some chicken raw meat pieces are shown in the following picture:

- Organs and eggs: liver, heart, kidney, green tripe (not the bleached kind in grocery stores), sweetbreads, etc. Heart, a muscle, is very rich and an important source of taurine for cats, which is an essential amino acid they do not produce internally—if you can not find fresh heart, you will need to provide a taurine supplement (which will be discussed later under supplements.)
- Vegetables: variety is key—mix above—and below-ground vegetables, predominated by green, leafy vegetables; **avoid onions and garlic completely**, as they cause some blood related problems for cats; also avoid too much of any one vegetable over time; can add small amounts of ripe fruit, seeds, nuts, parsley, herbs; avoid strong smelling vegetables.
- Add no-salt stock or broth or sprinkle with dried fish flakes to add flavor for finicky eaters.

As you can see, these are not complicated ingredients. They are all available at the grocery store. Planning to feed your cat is no more complicated than planning to feed your family. All you need is to add these items to your regular grocery list.

2. Supplements

Unless otherwise advised by your veterinarian, supplementation should be kept simple. Unless indicated by a specific condition that your cat has, you will only need to add a few vitamins and other additions to give your cat everything he needs. Keep in mind that the food itself provides a great deal of highly available vitamins and minerals from the raw meat and bones.

The basic supplements you will add to the diet are:

- vitamin B complex
- natural vitamin E
- kelp, dulse, and other seaweeds or grasses
- Omega-3 essential fatty acids from fish or salmon oil
- digestive enzymes
- probiotics

In most cases, these ingredients are added to commercial raw foods, so check labels to be sure they are present. Typically, frozen raw foods include more supplements than these base elements, which is fine, provided your cat does not have a reaction to any of those components. If you are feeding a commercial product and find your cat has a chronic reaction, you may be better off switching to Homemade or RMB Rotation options in order to have more control over ingredients.

You may choose to give vitamin C—some researchers believe that cats produce vitamin C naturally and do not need supplementation; others believe that it is a good idea. Since vitamin C is a water soluble vitamin, what is not used will be flushed out of the system.

Vitamin A is a critical component to the cat's diet. If you feed your cat a frozen prepared raw diet or make the recipe above, you will include enough raw liver to provide your cat with sufficient vitamin A. However, if you choose Option 4: RMB Rotation, you will need to be sure that you give sufficient liver to provide enough vitamin A. If you do not, you may want to add vitamin A supplement or cod liver oil to the cat's diet.[17]

Vitamins B and E are added to ensure that these critical vitamins are present in sufficient quantities. Kelp, dulse, and other seaweeds provide trace minerals such as iodine, selenium, etc. necessary for proper cell development. Seaweeds provide whole sources of these minerals so that your cat can benefit from them most readily.

Supplementing with Omega-3 essential fatty acids (EFAs) ensures that your cat is getting sufficient fats to produce healthy skin and coat, as well as ensuring he gets the proper balance of omega-six and omega-three essential fatty acids. This balance has proven important to long-term health in most mammals. Cats, as carnivores, do better with animal sources of EFAs than with plant sources; hence, your cat is likely to be able to digest salmon oil or fish body oil (not cod liver oil, which does not contain the right balance) more readily than flax seed, primrose, or borage oil, which are frequently used by humans and sometimes for dogs.

Digestive enzymes are especially important when first giving the raw diet, but may be used routinely, depending on the animal's needs. These are enzymes that contribute to digesting the food eaten. As your cat's system becomes more accustomed to eating the raw diet, you may choose to discontinue their use on a regular basis. For older animals, whose systems may be less efficient, continuing their use may be advised. Using digestive enzymes specifically designed for cats and dogs is recommended because their stomachs are so much more acidic than are humans, and hence are better suited to use for cats.

Probiotics are a fancy name for the good bacteria that populate the animal's intestines. They contribute to the digestive system's ability to absorb nutrients from food. They include acidophilus, lactobacillus and other good bacteria. In purchasing probiotics, look for those with in excess of 100 million live organisms.

Other supplements that may be given if desired include a mixed organ glandular supplement and colostrum. Some scientists believe that glandulars and colostrum are amazingly effective contributors to health.

In all these cases, it is strongly recommended that you read about the diet, learn about supplements, and consult with your veterinarian. Remember that every animal has different physiological needs and has different preferences for what he will eat, that food has varying degrees of nutritional value intrinsically depending on how and where it has been raised, and that you must feel confident that you are feeding your cat sufficient ingredients to support his health. In some cases, you will need to modify the recommendations made here to adapt to your cat's needs and tastes. Do not worry if your cat will not eat one particular item; simply keep in mind the principles and adjust to include other things that will provide the necessary component. Only you in partnership with your trusted veterinarian can attain the comfort you need to feed the raw diet reliably.

3. Final Note on Ingredients:

There are very few ingredients that can not be fed to your cat. He will tell you what he likes and dislikes, so pay attention to him and adjust accordingly. The more experience you gain and the more you learn about the raw diet and about supplements for animals, the more confidence you will have and the easier it will become. Start slow and simple, and don't worry—as long as you are providing sufficient variety over time, your cat will thrive.

Appendix

Resources

1. Annotated Bibliography

- **Bernard, Michelle T., *Raising Cats Naturally: How to Care for your Cat the Way Nature Intended*** (Blakkatz Publishing, date unknown.) One of the few books explicitly for cats, this book focuses on much more than diet. It does include recipes for feeding a raw diet to cats based on a recipe developed by Feline Futures. An excellent, if very detailed, description of how to feed cats a raw diet. Recommended for cat owners who want to understand the details, or for those who would like a recipe to make their own ground food.
- **Billinghurst, Ian, B.V.Sc. *Give Your Dog a Bone*** (Australia, 1993)—the premier book on feeding dogs raw meaty bones—it is a must-read for everyone feeding the BARF diet to their pets. It explains the principles underlying feeding this way and contrasts the results from raw feeding to those with commercially processed foods. It will be very important to read to understand the underlying concepts so you can feel comfortable with the amount of balance you're generating over time. But the book doesn't really help you figure out how to implement the diet. Strongly recommended.
- ——, ***The BARF Diet*** (Australia, 2001)—a follow-up to the first book, this one was written because so many people told him

they needed more guidance about feeding a raw diet. This is the book to start with and read before making the switch, since it clearly describes the underlying principles in a concise way and has specific, practical recommendations for feeding the diet. It is easy to read and full of great information. This book explains how to use the diet for both dogs and cats and distinguishes feeding puppies and kittens from adults. The only drawbacks are that it doesn't have the detail of the first book and it doesn't offer alternatives if making patties isn't your heart's desire. Highly recommended.

- ——, *Grow Your Pups With Bones* (Australia, 1998)—another follow-up to the first book, written largely to help people who want to breed healthy adults and wean puppies on a raw diet. It has much detail about the science underlying the nutritional aspects of breeding, whelping, and weaning, so it will be most useful if you breed your dog. Recommended if you are breeding your dog or want to learn more detail about young puppies.
- **Goldstein, Martin, DVM,** *The Nature of Natural Healing* (Alfred A. Knopf, 1999)—A wonderful book about animal health. It addresses diet thoroughly, but at the time it was written, Dr. Goldstein was not comfortable with the concept of raw meat and bone. Since then, he has completely come around and now endorses the BARF diet, so hopefully he will update his book soon. Nevertheless, this is a very worthwhile book to read to get a broader perspective on animal health and how you can promote it in your animals. It will give you more confidence that the raw diet is a great contributor to longevity and health. Strongly recommended.
- **Susan K. Johnson,** *Switching to Raw* (Birchrun Basics, 2001)—An excellent workbook style book that is the most practical guide out there for implementing a raw diet. This is another book to read before you make the switch. Use this book in conjunction with the Billinghurst or Schultze books because it has only a little bit of explanation but not enough to really understand they whys and hows of animal nutrition. What it *does* have that no other book does is practical recommendations for what

to feed when and how much, what the basic supplement are and how much to give, what to watch for, how to switch, and how to make the diet a regular practice. Has room for notes so that you can add what you learn as you follow it. Highly recommended.

- **Levin, Caroline D., RN,** *Dogs, Diet, and Disease: An Owner's Guide to Diabetes Mellitus, Pancreatitis, Cushing's Disease, and More* (Lantern Publications, 2001)—This book is written by a nurse who has a great deal of experience with these diseases in dogs and who writes about them clearly. One of her theses is that commercially produced dog food contributes to and exacerbates these diseases. She addresses the raw diet briefly and supports it although doesn't go into much detail. Most of the rest of the book deals with the care of dogs who have these diseases, and is an excellent source for anyone who owns such a dog. This book is recommended for anyone with a dog that has any of these diseases or who wants to learn more about the ways to prevent them through diet.

- **Lonsdale, Tom, DVM,** *Raw Meaty Bones: Promote Health* (Rivetco P/L, 2001)—A very detailed book that has a solid description of what is understood about animal nutrition from a scientific point of view. He is a tremendous advocate of feeding raw meaty bones because of the observations he has made as a practicing vet specializing in animal dental health. He is convinced that dental health contributes to health throughout the body, so this book combines a focus on the immune system support and the dental health support of the diet. The book is great if you want a more scientific approach, but is a little hard to wade through at times—he does a lot of advocacy for his point of view. Recommended for anyone wanting scientific explanations and experiment results explained.

- **MacDonald, Carina Beth,** *Raw Dog Food: Make It Easy for You and Your Dog!* (Dogwise Publishing, 2004)—A highly practical short book that addresses all the questions, issues, and concerns you might have without too much scientific or background material. Excellent for getting started. Recommended.

- **McKay, Pat,** *Reigning Cats and Dogs: Good Nutrition, Healthy, Happy Animals* (Oscar Publications, 1998)—Somewhat polemical, this book has easy-to-read descriptions of what to feed and what the ingredients contribute to the diet. It addresses some supplements that aren't examined elsewhere. Some of her claims aren't really justified globally—for example, she says not to feed chicken wings or legs because the bones may be problematic, but this will depend on the size of the dog and the chewing capabilities they have; most dogs, even puppies, will do just fine with whole wings and legs, and for smaller dogs, they can be chopped into pieces. She sells food so if you're interested in buying her product, reading this book may help understand her philosophy. Recommended as a supplement for those wanting to get a little more knowledge.
- **Puotinen, CJ,** *The Encyclopedia of Natural Pet Care* (Keats Publishing Inc., 1998)—A great all-around resource to have on the shelf, this book contains an excellent chapter on raw feeding. It explains some of the background that supports using the diet and also gives some good practical recommendations. This book, written by a frequent contributor to *The Whole Dog Journal*, is recommended as a resource and as a supplement to the other strongly recommended books.
- **Schultze, Kymythy R.,** *Natural Nutrition for Dogs and Cats: The Ultimate Diet*, (Hay House, Inc., 1998)—A short, very clear explanation of the raw diet with a lot of explanation about what nutrients are necessary. This book is a good alternative or supplement to the Billinghurst books and gives a little more practical advice. It gives good explanations of what to feed, how to switch, and how to address young and old animals' diets. It presents a monthly meal plan approach that is distinctive and may appeal to some. Also has great resource lists. Strongly recommended.
- **Segal, Monica,** *K9 KITCHEN—Your Dog's Diet: The Truth Behind the Hype*, (© Monica Segal, 2002)—An excellent straightforward, understandable book about dog nutrition, including detailed descriptions of the pros and cons of a raw diet. Includes nutritional analysis of raw meaty bones. Recommended for those interested in more nutritional detail.

WHOLE DOG JOURNAL Articles: Order back issues from *www.whole-dog-journal.com* or call 800-829-9165.

- **Kerns, Nancy, "The Meat of the Matter",** January 1999. Overview of raw feeding, addresses many concerns and objections, as well as offering resources similar to some of the other articles. A good starting point for considering getting started.
- **Puotinen, CJ, "Getting a Raw Deal: Why and how to convert your dog to a raw food diet",** September 1999. Talks about making the switch and gives excellent justification for the raw diet. A good starting place. Also lists resources for raw feeding.
- **Kerns, Nancy, "Food in the Freezer",** March 2000. Compares frozen raw diets and gives listing of ingredients, prices, comments, and contact information. Older than the Distenfeld article but a somewhat different group of resources.
- **"Raw Food Diet Does the Trick,"** June 2000. After drugs fail to cure his chronic itchiness, diarrhea, vomiting, and crankiness, a rescued Setter is transformed by good food!
- **"Practicing Safe Steaks,"** August 2000. Basic—but conscientious—food handling techniques keep meat healthy.
- **Thornton, Kim Campbell, "Bones of Contention",** September 2000. A great article describing the nutritional benefits of bones as well as potential dangers and how to balance the risks. A good read to understand why bones are so important as well as a realistic evaluation that will calm fears about bone safety.
- **Puotinen, CJ, "Raw-Fed Puppies",** December 2000. How to start puppies with a raw diet; all the reasons why to do so and how to do it. Great pictures of small puppies eating relatively huge bones successfully! List of breeders who wean their puppies on raw diets.
- **Puotinen, CJ, "Banking on Enzymes",** January 2001. Using enzymes to aid digestion and as systemic therapy; explains the whys and hows and tells how to give them to your dog.
- **Kerns, Nancy, "Comparing Raw Diet Plans",** June 2001. Compares Billinghurst, Shultze, and Volhard approaches to raw feeding.
- **Puotinen, CJ, "Feed Your Dog Back to Health",** September 2001. Discusses nutritional support for a variety of conditions,

particularly useful to supplement raw diets. Includes information on digestive enzymes, colostrum, probiotics, vitamins and minerals, etc. Has a good listing of resources for nutritional supplements.
- **Distenfeld, Rona, "Frozen Raw Diets",** May 2002. Description of various raw frozen diets available for sale. Great comparison table with source information, ingredient list, and analysis. If you're interested in buying raw food rather than making it, this is a must read. Only drawback is that not all foods will be available in your area. See also follow-up correction and addendum in June 2002 edition, **"More Frozen Raw Diets".**
- **"Store-Bought or Homemade?"** July 2002. The risks and benefits of commercial and home-prepared diets.
- **Kerns, Nancy, "Raw Information,"** September 2002. Discusses the advantages of raw feeding and also considers when raw feeding may not be recommended. The article shows that there are very few cases when raw feeding isn't preferred.
- **"Good Grinders,"** January 2003. Making dog food is easy and fast—when you have the right grinder.
- **Kerns, Nancy, "Mad Cow in Dog Food?"** July 2003. No immediate cause for alarm (but grass-fed beef looks better all the time.)
- **Puotinen, CJ, "What a Wolf Eats",** March 2005. Research on wild canids can help inform dietary planning for dogs.
- **Kerns, Nancy, "Completely Convenient,"** April 2006. Commercial frozen foods make feeding a "natural" raw foods diet easy.

2. Some Web-Based Resources

Information:
http://mysite.verizon.net/vze3k69i/—The story of my animals and our experience feeding a raw diet. Note: contact info on web site is not right
www.whole-dog-journal.com—The Whole Dog Journal web site; this is the "Consumer Reports" of dog products and training. An extremely valuable resource.
www.dogwise.com—Excellent source for dog books and other items.

www.barfworld.com—Ian Billinghurst's web site for information and selling food.
www.drianbillinghurst.com—Ian Billinghurst's practice web site.
http://home.earthlink.net/-affenbar—Kymythy Schultze's web site.
www.rawmeatybones.com—Tom Lonsdale's web site for his book and other information.
www.ahvma.com—American Holistic Veterinary Medicine Association website; locate a holistic vet in your area who is more likely to support raw feeding.
http://vetmedicine.about.com/cs/nutritionbarf/index.htm—good site to explore from.
http://www.k9rawdiet.com—a personal page with good information to share.
http://www.diamondpaws.com/health/barf.htm—a comprehensive source for books, information, products, etc.
http://www.leerburg.com/feedingdogs.htm—another source for all the recommended books and examples for dogs.
http://www.winnfelinehealth.org/index.html—a feline-specific research organization—a description of a raw feeding experiment and the effect on feline IBD can be found at *http://www.winnfelinehealth.org/reports/role-of-diet.html*
http://www.thebark.com—BARK magazine is not only a fun publication but also has many resources for raw food (most are located on the U.S. West Coast however.)

Food and Supplements:
www.b-naturals.com—excellent source for supplements, developed by Lew Olson, an animal nutritionist who advocates and teaches the BARF diet; highly recommended for vitamin supplements, digestive enzymes, probiotics, and seaweeds, and other supplements.
http://www.auntjeni.com/homemade.htm—source for frozen raw food with ground bone available in DC area; also sells excellent supplements, including probiotics and digestive enzymes, and all natural, non-grain based treats.
www.sitstay.com—good source for books, all natural dog treats, toys, all of excellent quality. Highly recommended (note: as of 1/1/07, this site no longer offers raw frozen food).

http://www.onlynaturalpet.com—great source for raw frozen and freeze dried food, among other all natural animal products.

http://www.bravorawdiet.com/—website for Bravo raw diet—excellent food, great source of information, helps you find distributors.

http://www.naturesvariety.com/—website for Nature's Variety food—be sure to look for Prairie (not Raw Instinct, which has grains); has some good information, allows you to find retailers. Also sells freeze dried varieties that are great for travel and emergencies.

http://www.primalpetfood.com/—website for Primal pet food—produces a cat specific chicken and salmon variety that is low in vegetables.

www.stevesrealfood.com—offers freeze dried BARF food—great for traveling or to keep on hand in emergencies—avoid the beef variety because it includes cooked bone meal, whereas chicken and turkey use backs or necks for bone

www.haretoday.com—sells frozen, whole ground animals, including bone, meat, and organs; varieties include chicken, turkey, rabbit, beef with green tripe, goat. Very fresh and well liked by picky cats; needs to have vegetables and supplements added.

www.iherb.com—iherb is a good source for supplements—they have a lot, are priced well, and ship quickly

http://www.animalessentials.com/index.html—a great source of animal-based supplements; they sell a calcium supplement made from seaweed (rather than cooked bone meal that is often used) that does not cause problems that bone meal does—if you aren't going to feed raw bone, then this is the best possible calcium supplement.

http://www.grizzlypetproducts.com/—great source of Salmon oil easy to dispense and add to meals

E-groups: Search for "barf" or "raw diet" to find more groups

Yahoo Groups—*www.yahoogroups.com*
Rawdiet
K9 Natural Diets
Barfdiet
Rrboot-camp
AdvBARF
SEVABarf

Smartgroups—*www.smartgroups.com*
BARFers
Barf Chat
Big Barf
Barfmentor

***Organic Farms*:**
Find local farms that produce pasture-raised animals by searching Google and looking at state and local extension websites.

Endnotes

1. For more information on the essential needs of cats, see *http://www.felinefuture.com*. See also Michelle T. Bernard, *Raising Cats Naturally* (Blakkatz Publishing, 2003).
2. The exception is eating grass—cats do not really digest the grass; it serves as a gut cleanser and may offer other benefits that are not related directly to digestion.
3. These problems evolve slowly over time, typically over the course of a year or two, but will eventually lead to serious physical problems.
4. This is not the only recipe that might be followed. Another good alternative can be found in Ian Billinghurst's book, *The BARF Diet*. Michelle Bernard includes a recipe similar to the one found here in her book, *Raising Cats Naturally*.
5. Naturally raised animals are typically (but not always, so check) fed a more natural diet (sometimes organic) that frequently includes higher quality nutrition, making their meat more nutritious for you and your cat. In general, these animals are not given antibiotics, steroids, or other growth promoting drugs. They are considerably more expensive than conventionally raised meat. Consider whether you are concerned enough about these differences to purchase the more expensive meat sources for your cat's food, and remember that whatever you decide, it will be better than feeding commercial, cooked food.
6. "Essential" amino and fatty acids are those that animals must obtain from their food because their bodies do not produce them on their own.

7 Doing the math for anyone who is concerned: a RMB is roughly one-third meat and two-thirds bone; RMB comprise 60% of the animal components, and meat comprises 30%, with organs/eggs as the remaining 10%. Multiplying out shows that this breakdown results in 50% meat, 40% bone, and 10% organs/eggs. Hence, when purchasing animal protein to use in making homemade cat food, it is helpful to consider grinding meat that is about half bone, half meat, since you will have to guess at the exact proportions. So, for example, in using a whole chicken, there may be considerably more meat than bone. To aim for these proportions, you may want to cut off some of the meat for your own dinner.

8 Various meat grinders are capable of grinding raw chicken and other poultry bones, although most manufacturers do not guarantee that they will grind bone. Suggestions for meat grinders are listed in the Appendix.

9 By including raw liver regularly in your cat's diet, you do not need to add a vitamin A supplement; liver is generally available, but if you are not able to get sufficient quantity, you may want to add a one or two teaspoons of cod liver oil to the recipe. Cod liver oil is high in vitamin A and also provides other vitamins, but is distinguished from fish body oil and salmon oil because it does not have the balance of Omega-3 fatty acids found in these oils. Using whole liver is always preferred to processed oil.

10 In general, it is preferable to include organs from the same animal breed as the raw meaty bones, e.g., use chicken liver and heart with chicken meat and bones. However, some varieties of organ meats are more readily available than others. The author believes that it is preferable to include whole organs rather than using supplements that include only part of the ingredient. Hence, if it is necessary to mix animal sources in order to include organs, that is preferable to relying on supplements. For example, if beef heart and liver are available but lamb heart and liver are not, in making a batch with lamb, use beef heart and liver rather than substituting taurine and vitamins A & D.

11 See www.FelineFuture.com.

12 Some research suggests that egg whites interfere with the body's ability to absorb biotin, an important B vitamin. Research on humans has shown that there must be a great deal of egg white

to interfere with biotin absorption. Similar research on cats is extremely limited. Whole eggs are used here for convenience and because it seems most natural that a cat in the wild would eat the whole egg, and two egg whites does not seem like enough to cause problems. If you are concerned about the egg white interfering with biotin absorption, simply use the egg yolks only.

13 Some researchers recommend against freezing probiotics and digestive enzymes; if this is a concern to you, or if your cat needs more digestive help, add them immediately before feeding.

14 Feline Futures recommends using a glandular supplement as a good way to get some of the components naturally produced in the organs of food animals. Consult your veterinarian for more information about what is appropriate for your cat's condition.

15 One drawback to buying already ground meat is that cats prefer meat to be very fresh. Once meat is ground, the surface area increases dramatically, increasing the opportunity for bacteria to reach it and begin the breaking it down. Even though we may not be able to smell any lack of freshness, cats seem to be able to and quickly reject meat that is not very fresh. Depending on how picky your cat is, you may find it preferable to grind the meat yourself.

16 This book does not intend to endorse any one particular product. However, finding calcium supplements that are not cooked and are suitable complements for the high-phosphorus content in a raw meat diet without grinding raw bones is difficult. Fortunately, *Animal Essentials* makes an excellent source of natural calcium from seaweed for dogs and cats that can be purchased in some pet food stores or can be ordered online at www.animalessentials.com. The author would welcome any information about other calcium supplements suitable to making raw cat food in this manner.

17 Billinghurst recommends cod liver oil in general, but Feline Futures does not recommend any source of vitamin A other than raw liver.

Made in the USA
Lexington, KY
17 September 2014